LESSONS WITH ED PARKER

2024 Edition

Lee Wedlake

Copyright © 2024 Lee Wedlake

All rights reserved, including the right to reproduce this book, or portions thereof in any form. No part of this text may be reproduced, transmitted, downloaded, decompiled, reverse engineered, or stored, in any form or introduced into any information storage and retrieval system, in any form or by any means, whether electronic or mechanical without the express written permission of the author.

The views expressed in this work are solely those of the author and do not necessarily reflect the views of the publisher, and the publisher hereby disclaims any responsibility for them.

Photos are from the author's collection unless otherwise noted.

ISBN: 978-1-917129-59-6

PublishNation LLC
www.publishnation.net

Dedication

To the students, instructors, and friends who were there to help make these events and experiences possible. They taught classes while I was away, went through the difficulties of having to re-learn things, and came along for the ride.

Acknowledgments

I would like to thank the following people for their help in making this book a reality; Phil Buck for the cover, Lance Soares, Bruce Meyer, Pete Tomaino, Steven White, Janis Nyman, John Sepulveda, the late Steve LaBounty, and the late Tom Kelly.

Table of Contents

Dedication i
Acknowledgments iii
Preface to the first edition by Bruce Meyer vii
Preface to the second edition by Lance Soares xvi
Foreword xx
Author's Note xxiii
What Happened? 1
November 13, 1979 – *First Lessons* 6
November 16, 1979 18
February 1980 – *Technical/historical/philosophical* 27
Summer 1980 – *First Chicago seminar* 53
June 16 - 21, 1980 – *Back to the future, the evolution of terminology* 58
November 1980 – *Teaching and training methods* 67
March 1981 – *The genesis of checking* 70
April 12, 1981 – *More zone theory* 72
May 1981 – *Knives, clubs, and Professor Chow* 86
February 23, 1982 – *Cover outs* 102
April 1982 – *He brought the 'chuks* 106
December 1982 – *Majors and minors* 124
May 1983 – *Style versus system* 130
November 1983 – *The basic forms* 133

May 1984 – *Multiple attackers and Form Four* 146

July 7-8, 1984 – *Wendy's® Martial Arts Seminars* 153

October 1984 – *Contouring and Form Five* 156

Jersey, Channel Islands, 1985 167

Mid-1980s – *My introduction to European Kenpo* 172

October 1985 – *Reinforcement* 175

Sydney, 1986 – *World-wide respect* 189

Chicago, September 1986 – *The Big Four seminar* 195

Australia, 1987 – *There's a riot goin' on* 204

The Late 1980s – *The Tribute, WLA, and more* 212

November 1990 – *The last seminar* 216

December 16, 1990 – *He's gone* 222

Memorable experiences 227

Other events, stories, and analogies – *Sam Ting, Sam Brown, and slow motion cigarettes* 251

The Audio Tapes – *More I had on cassette tapes recorded in my lessons* 274

February 12, 1980 275

February 13 and 14, 1980 279

June 18, 1980 282

Seminar 1980 285

November 1980 289

November 1981 292

Afterword 295

About the Author 301

Preface to the first edition

by Bruce Meyer

This book is about Lessons with Ed Parker and speaks for those of us fortunate enough to have even one lesson on the floor with the Senior Grand Master of the system, who heard the music in his Polynesian voice, and learned to dance the dances of death he created for us. For those of us who saw him move, a blur of silver and black and who experienced the thunder of his hammers, or felt the flashing of his wings; for those of us who felt the lifting of our feet from the floor as his perfectly placed kick launched us into the air at the end of a grueling promotion test.

Those of us that can tell you "the story about the time Ed Parker" did this or said that, had the reality of how few and precious those moments were driven home on December 15, 1990 when he arrived home in Hawai'i and then was taken away. Those of us, who have even one story to tell about getting rocked by the old man, can tell you where we were when we got rocked by the news of his passing.

This book is about those times, those lessons. Those times were good times. You can see it in the faces of those who tell their stories about a lesson with Ed Parker.

This book is also for those that never had the opportunity to have had a lesson with Ed Parker. In this book Lee Wedlake takes us into both the public and private aspects of lessons with Mr. Parker, opening up his private notebooks to share with you his experiences and thoughts of those lessons.

I was at a Saturday seminar recently at which I described to the students there Mr. Parker's creative mind. I told them about how he had created all of the techniques and forms and how the gray in their Kenpo Crest patch represented Mr. Parker's brainpower. Afterwards a young orange belt girl about 10 years old said to me, "I wish I could have met Mr. Parker."

For those that have that same wish, Mr. Wedlake has written this book. Some of the stories in this book will make you laugh, and some will give you cause to meditate on your own journey in Kenpo and life. Thanks to him you now have the opportunity to catch the words and thoughts of the Senior Grand Master himself.

We that had the opportunities to be there, you can almost hear his voice. If you ever had the chance to hear him laugh and see him smile your own memories of Lessons with Ed Parker will be awakened. Yeah, this book is for all of us.

This portion of the introduction is about Lee Wedlake. Every master creates his or her disciples. Those who see their vision, share their dreams, and accomplish shared goals. Among those disciples there is always the development of various disciplines based upon each ones interpretation of their experiences with the master and seasoned by their individual talents and lives. A cursory reading of the New Testament Gospels teaches us this. Each of the four Gospels gives us a different view of the man, Jesus. Many items in each of these four manuscripts, from accounts of his birth, death and resurrection may even seem to contradict things written in the others. Yet all are about the same man. As did his Master, Jesus the Christ, so did Senior Grand Master Ed Parker.

I have had the opportunity to train with many of "the best" in Parker Kenpo during my time starting from those first years of working my way through the colored belts. Learning the next technique or form are still memories that I can draw on at will. One of those strongest memories was as a green belt reading the introduction of Ed Parker's *Infinite Insights into Kenpo, Volume 3*. That was when my soul ran into the name of Lee Wedlake.

I remember sitting in my den that evening in Lakewood, California. I had purchased the book two days previous but based upon a lesson I had learned from Joe Hyams' book, *Zen and the Martial Arts*, I waited until I had the time to relax and open my soul to this book. I continue to recommend *Infinite Insights into Kenpo, Volume 3* to all those who train with me. From its first words regarding teamwork you can feel Mr. Parker's appreciation for those who shared his dream. I memorized the colored belt pledges and have sought to make them a part of my own personal creed to life. Yeah, even in those words the Old Man got it right. I remember reading the dedication to a man I had never met, Bernie Bernheim, and hoping to become such a man. Then, I remember reading the preface of that book. As I read, it described to me many things including a brief description of Ed Parker and his accomplishments, a history of the martial arts and Kenpo in the United States, and a concise explanation of the checking principles that was then and still is one of the defining differences between the Parker System and many traditional systems. In the preface I found described to me two very important ideals. One was a description of the type of martial art that I wanted to master. The second and as equally important to me was the kind of martial artist I wanted to become. That preface was my introduction to the writings of Lee Wedlake. I put the book down to meditate on what I had read. A quick thought occurred that some day I hoped to meet him and tell him what I thought of what he had written.

Over the next few years I came across more of Lee's writings as they appeared in various martial arts publications. Every time I read something new it was like having had a private lesson. His explanations of details and principles provided clarity. I came across his article entitled *Brace Yourself* in *Karate International Magazine*. After reading it, I went back through all of the techniques and applied the principles described in the article.

When Mr. Parker died I was pleased to see Lee Wedlake's name in *Black Belt* magazine as the author of the memorial article. It was an informative and inspirational piece and I recall thinking then that Mr. Parker must have felt pleased with Lee's work. Once again I was inspired by the writings of a man that I had not yet met.

In 1993 with the help of my wife, Alice and our son Paul, I opened my own Kenpo Karate studio in South Carolina. It was soon after that I had my first opportunity to meet Mr. Wedlake at Sean Kelly's studio in Greenacres, Florida.

We had a fantastic weekend of Kenpo. Frank Trejo was there working sticking hand drills, Huk Planas went over

Form Five, and Lee covered the two man attack techniques; Marriage of the Rams and Snakes of Wisdom with various combinations of the two. I never had so much fun getting bruised up in my life. During that weekend I had a few chances to speak with Mr. Wedlake one to one. I bought a fresh copy of *Volume 3* and after telling him how greatly it had impacted my martial arts training, I asked him to sign it for me. As he signed the book it was like the fulfillment of a projected moment in time. Déjà Vu forward, if you will. When he handed it back to me he thanked me for telling him how much the words he had written in it had mattered to me. He shook my hand and in that instant a bond was formed that I know will last until we both are gone from this life.

I extended an invitation to him to come to my school for a weekend training session and within a couple of months he was able to come. What a fantastic weekend that was. He came up a day early just to hang around. Back then I was just starting aviation ground school and I made arrangements for us to rent a Cessna and go flying for a while. I can still remember the look on the guy's face when he asked Lee to see his license. "Yes, I guess you know how to fly a Cessna" was all he had to say as he handed back the wallet. It still makes me laugh whenever I think about it.

We flew around for a while and had a great time, culminating in my taking the controls for the first time in my life.

That evening we tested one of my brown belts, Nick Dreiling, for black belt. At one point Mr. Wedlake asked him a very interesting question about a couple of moves in Form Four. He asked, "Why do you do" that particular move? Now that was a new thought. I knew for sure how to do the move but I had never yet thought of why! In that moment, with that simple word, "why", a whole new world of Ed Parker's Kenpo opened up to me and to my students.

Later that evening, while sitting in my living room, we began to relax and to talk about our various martial arts experiences. We both laughed when we discovered that the very first martial arts book that ether of us had ever read was Bruce Tegner's *Complete Book of Karate*. I had a copy of it on my bookshelf and showed it to him.

As the next day's sessions progressed I watched Lee instructing my students and listened to him as he taught. I heard him relate so many experiences that he had with Mr. Parker. My students learned not just the hows and the whys of Kenpo, but they received something just as precious; they received a history lesson of their art. They listened as

Lee told them some of the same episodes that you will read about in this book.

Later that evening we took a stroll around the historic Capitol grounds of Columbia, South Carolina. We walked up the marble steps of the capitol building. I showed him the five bronze stars on the building wall that marked the spots where General William Tecumseh Sherman's cannon balls had scarred it. It was a perfect South Carolina night. We happened past an old Methodist Church cemetery and Lee inquired if we could walk through it to look at some of the ancient grave stones. After a while we separated and when I relocated him, he was standing before an old headstone with a look of wonder. As I walked up to him he looked at me and then pointed to the marker. "Ed Parker" was the name on the stone. The moment was so surreal.

As we were sitting by the fireplace that night I told him that I felt that he was uniquely qualified to write about Mr. Parker. In his humility he responded that he wasn't sure. Many years have passed since that night. Since then I have not only become a student and disciple of Lee Wedlake, I have become a friend and one of those close enough to call him brother.

In these ensuing years he has written many books defining and explaining the system that we uphold. In this aspect, more then any other disciple of Mr. Parker, Lee Wedlake has "Kept the Flame Burning." In his previous books, just as in his earlier magazine articles he has provided enlightenment into the concepts and principles of Ed Parkers Kenpo.

This book is different. Now that the hows and whys have been covered in his previous books, Mr. Wedlake takes you, his reader, into a different realm. In this book you will get to know more about the Zen lessons that come from times off the training floor with Mr. Parker. Here Lee opens up a new view into the heart and humor of Ed Parker.

Lessons with Ed Parker is the book that I always hoped Lee would write. I am sure that Lee must have felt Mr. Parker's spirit sitting next to him many times while he wrote this book, because I sure felt it as I read it.

Thanks Lee, for everything.

Bruce Meyer
Fifth degree black belt
Columbia, South Carolina

Bruce has kept training and is a seventh degree.

Preface to the second edition

by Lance Soares

Embarking upon the pages of this second edition of "Lessons with Ed Parker," readers are poised to engage in an extraordinary exploration that transcends conventional martial arts narratives. Guided by the discerning hand of Lee Wedlake, this isn't merely a compilation of Kenpo lessons but a profound venture into the very essence of Ed Parker—a figure whose influence extends far beyond the confines of the martial arts community. It has been over three decades since Mr. Parker's departure, and in an era now marked by the scarcity of people who had personal encounters with him, this book presents a rare opportunity to intimately connect with the martial arts icon. This book emerges as a cherished bridge spanning temporal gaps.

Venture into the personal dimension of Ed Parker through narratives woven by one closely acquainted with him. Gain profound insights into Parker's multifaceted life as a martial artist, a father, a grandfather, and a cherished friend. Within these pages, the reader is invited to vicariously experience Mr. Parker's impact through the perspectives of those who shared intimate moments with him.

The author's prose aspires to paint a vibrant and nuanced portrait of Ed Parker. This work transcends the conventional boundaries of martial arts literature; it serves as a jubilant celebration of Parker's humanity, portraying him not merely as a pioneer in martial arts but as a relatable figure with a rich personal history.

For those unacquainted with the founder of American Kenpo methodology, "Lessons with Ed Parker" serves as an enlightening initiation. It is not a mere instructional guide and it offers a transformative journey into the heart of a visionary who indelibly shaped the landscape of martial arts.

Contained within these pages are personal anecdotes and stories, providing glimpses into the private moments and interactions that defined Ed Parker's legacy. Among these, a particularly poignant moment unfolds through the story of a 14-year-old yellow belt—myself. At a seminar with Ed Parker Sr. in early 1987, I vividly recall sizing up what I considered an 'old man.' Little did I know that this 'old man' would turn out to be a martial arts legend.

Drawing upon personal experiences and those of others, the author brings to life pivotal moments that underscore Mr. Parker's indelible impact. From the perspective of a 14-year-old yellow belt to the seasoned martial artist and instructor I've become, the author adeptly highlights the enduring legacy of lessons learned directly from Ed Parker himself.

Readers are not only treated to glimpses of Mr. Parker's character but also offered insights into the interconnected web of martial arts history. The author emerges as a bridge between past and present, providing not just lessons but a living connection to the roots of Kenpo.

In my years of studying under Mr. Wedlake, we have engaged in fascinating conversations about his interactions with Mr. Parker. These discussions provided me with a valuable insider's perspective, revealing the depth of thought and history that shaped the evolution of this martial art.

Acknowledging the challenge of preserving history for a new generation of practitioners who never had the chance to meet Ed Parker, this book becomes a compelling call to action. Embrace the journey into the heart and mind of a true martial arts pioneer. "Lessons with Ed Parker" is not merely a book but a vessel for the transmission of knowledge, ensuring that the legacy of Ed Parker remains vibrant and relevant for generations to come.

Lance Soares, Senior Professor
Massachusetts, USA

Foreword

I was asked if I would ever write a book on Ed Parker's life. Part of my response was that his life is pretty well documented and much of what I would write would be easily found elsewhere. What I was planning to do was write down the parts of his life in the last years that I was personally involved in, and that's what this book is about.

My old videos of Ed Parker seminars I had hosted in Chicago back through the 1980's needed to be preserved, so I transferred them to DVD. Many had been shot with a cheap black and white video camera, the only thing I could afford back then. The technology was relatively new for home use and expensive. Today's cameras are way better and cost less. But I'm glad I had that camera because I was able to capture Ed Parker teaching many aspects of Kenpo in what was to be the last decade of his life.

I had made a promise to him back then. When I asked if I could tape him teaching he said "Yes, but under one condition". That condition was that I was not to make copies for anyone without his permission. I had a few ask and I remember him giving the go ahead once or twice. But you won't or shouldn't find clips of him from Chicago on the Internet, and that's why.

All these years I've had all those tapes in boxes and people have asked if I would copy them and I've refused. I've been enticed by some, telling me how much money I could make by selling them. I could not reconcile my promise to him with the prospect of making money on the tapes. I'd be breaking my word.

On the other hand, if they sat in a box, would I be depriving the Kenpo world of another asset to perpetuating our art? The argument was made that seniors like me would teach what he taught and so, I should keep them to myself. And while I would not copy them I <u>could</u> show them to my students. And I did. Each time they made the same remarks about how cool it was to hear his voice and to watch him move. His stories and mannerisms excited them just as he excited my generation of students. I just didn't know what to do with the videos. I would eventually upload them to the Web, in such a manner they can be watched but not downloaded. At this writing they are on my pages at www.vimeo.com. They are accessed by subscription. In two tiers, one for beginners and another for instructors and advanced ranks.

I wrote the first edition of this book before deciding to upload the seminar videos. While you won't see him move, you will read what he had to say in those seminars, in his words. You'll also read what he imparted to me in my private lessons, which I recorded on a small tape recorder and on a yellow tablet. Hopefully you'll get as much out of those notes as I did and not think of this as the ramblings of an old instructor. That's why I call this book *Lessons <u>with</u> Ed Parker*, not *Lessons <u>from</u> Ed Parker*. It was not a matter of him lecturing us or talking <u>at</u> me in my lessons. It was interactive in seminars, and often a discussion in the private lesson. I'd say his *Infinite Insights* series are the lessons from, along with his other books. In this book I'd like you to feel like you're there, learning with us. He was learning, too and you could see it from time to time, the delight in discovery, and his excitement to share it. Come along with us.

Lee Wedlake

Author's Note

Ed Parker was frequently referred to as "The Old Man". As the crew calls a ship's captain by that, so it was that we would refer to him. It was done with no disrespect and I use it in this book in the same manner. I miss him every day.

Much of what he said directly to me is in italicized quotes. I have done minimal editing so you can get more of the flavor of his phraseology and that may help you understand him better. Other quotes from seminars are in standard format.

In addition, he covered much of the same material over the years. Surely because it bore repeating, maybe because he used a "canned" format and at times he was tired and fell back to the tried and true presentations. Due to that the same stories and analogies would be told at different times. He basically taught the same seminar I attended in 1979 in California that he did in Chicago many times, and other places I went with him. In Chicago I usually had a beginner seminar in which he taught the aforementioned seminar and then had him do an advanced class on various subjects. Most of the senior people would attend both. I have tried to be true to the timeline. Trivia buffs may want to know that *seminars were two hours in length and sometime in the late 1980s became 1.5 hours after discussing attention spans, sore feet and backs. However, Ed Parker always ran over the two hour mark.*

He frequently used the Socratic Method in his teaching in that he'd answer a question with a question. When he spoke he'd often insert a rhetorical "what?" into a sentence. For example, he'd say, "Keeping your hand up gives you what?" Then a pause, and he'd continue with the answer. His talks were also interspersed with such phrases as "in terms of" and "whereby". And he loved to tell the group to "Try this on your mother-in-law" to get a laugh. As you read the book I hope you'll get an idea of his personality, presentation, attitudes, and sense of humor.

In addition, with this revision, I have added material not found in the first edition. In late 2023 I digitized the cassette tapes of voice recordings I made during my lessons. They had been stored for about 40 years and I was surprised and pleased to find they were undamaged and still played. I bought a converter and as I listened I wrote notes about those lessons and have added chapters about their content.

Some historical context was needed too. What was happening in the industry in the 80s? What did he say about the business aspects? Who came on the scene in that time?

He was in the process of rebuilding the IKKA and training those he would later name as his proteges. What about the fragmentation of the IKKA after he passed?

At this writing it is 33 years since he passed. We have at least two generations of Kenpoists who either never met him and some who don't know who he was. It has become difficult for some to determine who was there. I was told once that he "Has more students now than when he was alive". I read web postings with claims they studied with him or give a strong impression that they did. I know many of these people and know for a fact they did not. Today they wear a belt with IKKA style markings, wear a patch similar to the crest, and even state on video that he was their instructor. I have called out some who have and they have retracted the statement. I do such things in private, not on social media.

There are still enough seniors who legitimately studied with Ed Parker for one to verify lineage. Many have passed and the rest of us are not getting younger. I was told recently that I am "the last of the first", the last of the first generation students. You'll read their names within. Keep in mind that some making claims today actually were trained by one of us but name Ed Parker as their teacher. Some learned the material off a print-out or video and the "polishing up" that was to follow never happened. Some of them write the teacher who trained them out of their history and point to another as their instructor. Please, give credit where due. I found "shoppers" jumping lineages, some being collectors who changed affiliations to get a certificate and often a quick promotion, or even a double promotion.

Seeing all that and watching video posted online, one can see the loss of application of Parker principles in technique and forms. I see the very mistakes he demonstrated as being dangerous to us still being repeated today. Ideas he inserted into the sequences have been either not taught, misinterpreted or ignored. I see 5th degree blacks who can't even hit an attention stance or retract a kick in a form. It makes me wonder why I've spent so much of my life traveling, writing and teaching. Then I see the ones who get it. The effort has been worth it. The art is in good hands with many. My perspective changed over years and it changed my teaching. Mr. Parker knew it. He'd say "Pair up and good luck", knowing most would go right back to doing what they knew. If this was easy, everyone would do it.

Photo by Brad Crooks

What Happened?

Chicago, November 2023 seminar.
There are seven men here who attended Ed Parker seminars more than once. Kurt Barnhart, Dennis Pratl, Rick Vecchi, Ed Bilski, Jon Landin, Duane Shue and Terry Ward.

Ed Parker used to like to say there are three types of people in the world. The first makes it happen, the second waits for it to happen, and the third says, "What happened?" Ed Parker was a make-it-happen guy. I am too, and I think he saw that in me. He would say he liked to come to Chicago to teach because everything was so organized.

I had met him at the International Karate Championships (IKC) in Long Beach in 1977.

We again crossed paths at some national tournaments. I was competing a lot and in 1979 had earned enough points to make the National Top Ten. He must have been watching. In August that year, my teacher at the time, Mike Sanders, died in a motorcycle accident. Mr. Parker remembered him. In fact, in 1978 he had introduced me to Mills Crenshaw, who had been Mike's teacher back in the 60s in Salt Lake City. At a later event in Cleveland, Ohio Mr. Parker asked me to meet him after the tournament. It was there he said, "When can you come to California?" I told him whenever he wanted me there I'd be there. He continued to tell me that what he intended to do was teach a handful of protégés from around the country and he wanted me to represent him in the Midwest. The certificate below shows that happened the weekend of September 8, 1979.

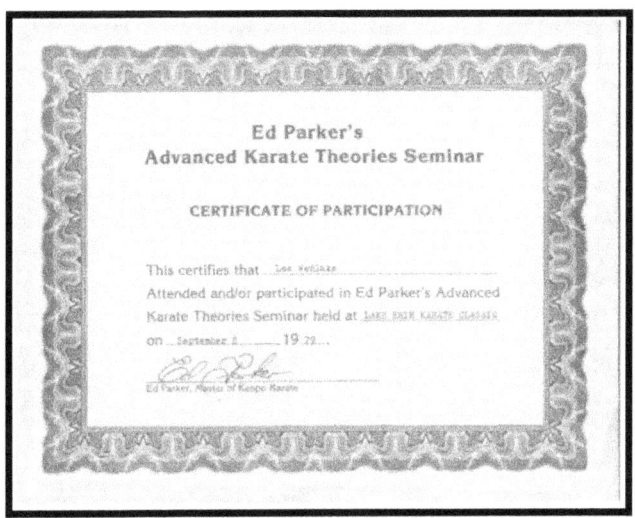

By November I found myself in Pasadena, California at the headquarters school taking private lessons directly from "The Father of American Karate".[1]

I met him at the studio and as he taught me the benches filled with spectators, lots of black belts. They were respectful and quite intent. After this he told me "I'm teaching you, not them. Meet me at the house." That was

---

[1] It was *Inside Kung-fu* magazine in its May 1974 issue (p. 9) that gave him that name. He told me "I never asked for it. It was a magazine that hung it on me." I have a copy of the magazine. *Black Belt*, the February 1975 issue, also refers to him by that title.

how I became one of his private students at his home. The subsequent lessons were at his house and that's where I took many of the notes I want to pass along to you.

So, what happened that led up to this? First, I used my limited resources to travel and compete, wanting to make my system and my teacher look good. Sanders had been encouraging, and he worked me hard while giving me what I needed to excel. He was tough, and not one to give compliments for compliments sake. You were as likely to get punched in the chest as get a "Nice job" from Mike. I traveled 120 miles each way to train with him as often as possible and he came to my little studio in Palos Hills, Illinois to work with my students. I wasn't a person who took a five-minute drive to the studio twice a week because Mike was the only Parker black belt in northern Illinois.

Second, I made myself known to Ed Parker and wasn't afraid to talk to him. I respected him and didn't follow him around like some others, but I got out there, did my art, and he noticed. I called him when Mike passed away. However, I never really thought I'd get the opportunity to train privately with the Grandmaster. You could have knocked me over with the proverbial feather when he asked me to come to California.

My experience is a combination of skill, hard work, follow-through, a lineage, being in the right place at the right time, and some luck. The result was the chance of a lifetime to work with one of the most famous martial artists in the history of American Karate, if not martial arts in general. That's what happened. Today I see this in others. Ed Parker took his time to meet me at his studio and then take me under his wing by teaching me at the house and coming to Chicago for seminars. I have done the same for those showing the desire because this art is to be shared. What happened to me can happen to the next generation of Kenpo students, if they want badly enough to train with the person they perceive as the master.

The First Private Lesson

November 13, 1979

The Basics

I vividly remember my first formal lesson with Mr. Parker. I showed up at the Pasadena studio and I was nervous. I had flown out from Chicago the day before and had arranged to stay for a week. Frank Trejo was managing the studio for Mr. Parker and later I realized he was checking me out to see if I'd make the cut. Lots of people were banging on Ed Parker's door to get into his circle. This was a bit unusual for a guy like me to get invited. I was fortunate to have Mr. Trejo to show me the ropes. Later Frank would tell me I was the "best of the bunch" that came in the front door from other places. He had tales of all kinds of flakes, wackos, and sub-standard practitioners.[2] Of

---

[2] Trejo was in a photo with Ed Parker in the December 1979 issue of *Inside Kung Fu* magazine that came out in November. I had met Frank a year or so before when I went to the Internationals and stopped at the Pasadena studio. When I introduced myself I said, "I'm Lee Wedlake from Chicago", and Frank responded with, "Yeah, so what?"

course there were lots of good ones too and we're proud to wear the Pasadena patch.

When Mr. Parker came in we quickly got started. The school was almost empty because it was a weekday morning. He showed me how to salute in the way he wanted it done. Being an "off-shoot" I had a semblance of the way he wanted it done but he made sure I got it right. Then it was "Down in your horse".

In the first few minutes I realized that while I had learned and improved quite a bit under the tutelage of Mike Sanders in Illinois, what I had learned did not have the depth I would get from Ed Parker.

Stances

My original hand-written notes on lined yellow paper have stances, maneuvers, blocks, strikes, and others listed as being the Five Basic Categories. We started with stances and in the side column it is marked "#1 Stances". In the basics prioritization stances are the first element taught because, as we say, Rule #1 is to establish your base.

For years I thought about how he labeled the basics lists in the requirements booklets as Basic Fundamentals. It seemed to me that basics were fundamental and the term was redundant. I realized that his lists were actually of the basics of the basics.

There was discussion of the neutral bow stance, fighting horse, and close and wide kneel stances. He made a point of the fighting horse as being pigeon-toed versus the 45-degree, feet-parallel, position in the neutral bow. The fighting horse was his favorite stance. I believe this was because he liked the way his feet gripped the ground with the toes turned in and how the muscles in the lower leg are engaged differently than in the neutral bow. This same idea is used in the forward bow stance and is a big reason why we keep our front foot turned inward. Most systems have their front foot straight and I've only seen two or three other systems do what we do.[3] If you pull on an extended arm of a person standing in a solid stance with the front foot straight as in the forward leaning stance many use, you can pull them off balance. If you try the same thing on someone with the front foot turned in it is much more difficult.

He told me that his terms of "wide" and "close" were established using the knees as the points of reference when he labeled the wide and close kneel stances. My note says "not depth". It seems many get confused, using depth as the

---

[3] Hung Gar, and one tai chi system.

measure, rather than width. Wide and close refer to side-to-side, not front-to-back.

We then went through the cat, twist, diamond and concave stances. He spent time on the Margin for Error principle as it related to stances and the dimensions of height, width, and depth with an emphasis on the correct positions of toe-heel and heel-knee lines to get proper height. It was an introduction to tailoring, an element so important to the practice of the arts, and to the art of living life.

Leg and body maneuvers

We then moved on to #2 as marked on my notes. I have 2a -Leg, and 2b – Body, written next to a list of the shuffles and foot maneuvers. The four shuffles are listed and the step-through, shuffle, jump-leap-hop, cover and switches are in another column.

He elaborated on the cover, the small foot maneuver we use to turn and face the obscure zone. It should be noted that the term is also used to refer to a hand position, often called a position check, and to the cover-out maneuver, used to move away from an opponent at the end of a technique. The term here is used in reference to the foot maneuver.

"Always move the lead leg to move away from action – increase protection and dissipate force" is what I wrote down. "Reason: forward leg which is shifting drops you back and away from unknown action – aids in nullifying the effectiveness of opponent's efforts in creating distance and decelerates his action." Mr. Parker was emphatic in teaching that you "never move toward the unknown". It was a statement heard time and again by students and is taught today. I would say that there are times you may move toward the unknown and that the teaching is certainly valid when introducing the concept at the beginner level. An advanced student may find a situation where it is necessary to move into the unknown.

We went on to switches, the three main types. He simply described them as moving your front leg back then back leg forward; moving your rear leg forward then front leg back, and jumping in place. It was interesting to see how he later changed the names by which he referred to the switches. At this first lesson they were called front-leg-to-rear-leg, rear-leg-to-front-leg, and jump switches. As time progressed the first two were called front-to-back and back-to-front. He defined them as bringing your front foot to your rear foot and vice-versa. Later he would name them by direction, that is, when you brought your front foot back it was a back-to-front switch because you went back before going forward and the other was front to back because you went forward before going back. This caused some confusion with many people. Today I call them front-foot-to-rear-foot and rear-foot-to-front-foot switches because the name tells you exactly what you are to do.

We then went into body maneuvers such as bobbing, weaving, slipping, and riding the force. It is interesting to note that the first three are not on a basics list, or at least they were not on the lists back then. He wanted us to be familiar with them and he discussed them with me. They are mentioned in his *Infinite Insights* books but they are not in the techniques. Riding the force is the only element that is and it shows up in such techniques as *Triggered Salute* and *Leap from Danger*.

Blocks and parries

These are marked as #3 in my notes. Over the years I developed a name for the categorization of the basics I call the "Basics Priority". It is based on what he taught me in that stances are number one, because you need a base to work from. Blocks are second and parries are third. They both need a base to work from, each in their own way. When the attack is redirected we can hit back by either 4) punching, 5) striking or, 6) using finger techniques. Then we can think about whether to kick or maneuver, each of which takes more balance. He interchanged their position in the priority from time to time with the kicks being first because of their reliance on balance or the maneuvers due to their being in motion. Today I tell my students it doesn't really matter which one is #7 or #8 as long as they know about the priority.

He differentiated striking blocks and parrying blocks. A striking block is in direct opposition to the force and a parrying block rides the force. Today we say blocks oppose and parries ride but there are hybrid moves that are either more of a block than parry or parry than a block. In general we also say that blocks are with the hands closed and parries with the hands open. Therefore we have blocking parries and parrying blocks. The downward diagonal block in *Deflecting Hammer* is a parrying block. The upward parry in *Circles of Protection* is a blocking parry. These examples illustrate those gray areas of application.

What he called a position block was your guard, "a defensive position in anticipation of defense when action is taken." He would later refer to that as a cover or position check. There is a difference in both the cover and the position check, with the cover being in anticipation and the check in actual use. The definition of a check includes hindering, repressing, or restraining. I believe his ideas were constantly being refined, and so were his definitions. It comes as no surprise that my notes are somewhat different, due to that refining and changing, and also my perceptions of what he said. However, in defense of myself, I need to say that he had me transcribe my notes into typewritten form for him so he could crosscheck them. Much of this information found its way into the *Insights* series in such a way. At that time Mr. Parker was working on the *Infinite Insights into Kenpo* book, which wasn't originally supposed to be five volumes, and he asked me (and others like me) to transcribe notes from the lessons and send them to him. It was a clever way to get the material written down and give him triggers for what needed to be included in the book(s). It was a process he would use for years while he finished the series.

Pinning, hugging, and specialized blocks were also covered. The specialized blocks were "moves employing several of the above in application." Examples were trapping combinations, blocks that grabbed, jammed, or caught the attack. He defined a catch as capturing a weapon in flight and a grab as having continued control of that weapon. Some systems catch the punch then bend the wrist to affect a lock. We will catch and grab a kick, more so in some of the older techniques that are not on the post-1970 lists.

Strikes

Section #4 in my notes is on strikes with the arms, hands, legs, and feet. He was definite in stating that kicks were strikes with the legs and feet but deserve their own category. He said there were fine distinctions between punches and strikes. We usually say if we hit with the front of the first two knuckles it is a punch. If we hit with other surfaces, it's a strike. Frank Trejo loved to confound students with the saying that you can strike with a punch but you can't punch with a strike.

He introduced me to the methods of execution. My notes show thrusting, slicing, clawing, whipping, roundhouse, and hooks. For some reason, hammering isn't in there. Later we would teach the four <u>basic</u> methods as hammering, thrusting, whipping, and slicing. Roundhouse, hook, and claw were the "other three". All students should be familiar with the first four.

In one of the audio tapes, he states there is an eighth, that being specialized methods such as lifting and looping.

Specialized moves

Another name for some of these is "exotic basics", a term used by Huk Planas. This is where we find in section #5 the mentions of tackling, butting, sandwiching, grappling, and vice-like moves. As a former football player, Ed Parker was not opposed to tackling. He told me a story of meeting with Bruce Lee. I don't know if it was the first meeting but they were "hands-on". He said Bruce went into his traditional Wing Chin guard stance, which is a kind of rear bow stance with most of the weight on the back leg and the front leg almost straight. He said he checked off the lead hand and went into a rolling body block he learned in football, taking out Lee's front leg and causing him to fall. It was after that, according to him, that "Bruce Lee changed his fighting stance." If you research it, you'll see that Bruce Lee did change from the back stance to a strong side forward stance that looks like our close kneel stance. I'm not saying he got the stance from Ed Parker, just that he changed.

Head butts are always good and they show up here and there in the system. Ed Parker liked sandwiching, too. Not only with the heel-palm/elbow combination but by slamming people into walls, the ground, other people, etc. to effect a sandwich. There is a lot of stand-up grappling in

Parker Kenpo, and the head butt strikes are integrated, plus he told me there was a ground system.

Vice-like moves included some types of sandwich, as well as breaking combinations and biting.

At this point he spoke of intermittent power. This was my introduction to majors and minors. I was familiar with the idea but he made it much more defined and clearer to me. My note says, "Major power combined with minor strikes". I wrote down minor moves as "set-up" with blocks, whips, slices, and rakes next to it. Next to major I wrote "most damaging blows". I like to use the example of a finger whip to the eyes followed by a punch or straight heel-palm.

The next two days I worked with the late Frank Trejo, who taught me the yellow belt techniques, and which must have been a bore for him. I appreciate everything Frank did for me then, and over the years. He was a brother. And one of the best practitioners we had.

So here I was, a hotshot second-degree black belt with a bunch of tournament wins in fighting, forms and weapons and some street fighting experience and I was going from Square One. Essentially my first lessons with Ed Parker were almost the same as the lessons a white belt would get. There was more detail, of course, but that was why I was there and I loved every minute. I had known <u>how</u> and not as much <u>why</u>. Mike had done a pretty good job with me, but there were still holes in my knowledge.

Something Ed Parker said to me later, and he wrote it in what was to be a preface to my first book, *Kenpo Karate 101,* was that he thought it was important that I was willing to go backward to move forward and he respected that. The Chinese classics have a saying to that effect when they say, "To go forward you must go backward". I'd have taken off my belt and put on a white belt after that first lesson. Many a person has come into my schools as a black belt and told me the same thing after their first lesson. It's the old "empty your cup" thing. If you think you know it all you're probably not going anywhere.

Private lesson

November 16, 1979

This was when I started working the techniques with Mr. Parker. We began with the orange belt material. My first notes indicate that I had been missing the effect of the downward/inward clearing angles we do in so many techniques that is introduced in *Lone Kimono*.[4] That angle controls height and width and prevents the opponent from countering you with a head butt whether intentional or unintentional. In the versions of Kenpo I had previously learned there was no mention of this idea. However, when I trained with Mike Sanders he pointed out that he always had the hands in place to prevent such actions and so made the structure/sequence of the techniques different. In the first offshoot system I originally learned there was no

---

[4] So many of us have a *Lone Kimono* story involving a head butt from a bad clearing angle. He'd use it to illustrate angle of cancellation. More often than not, when he'd go into detail on a technique, he had a habit of leaning on his "victim" with one hand on their shoulder while standing in a one-legged crane stance as he described his points. He did this often and it always felt good, like he was saying "I like this guy."

mention or use of such checks or angles of cancellation. I was to find that if I did those techniques I had originally learned (e.g. *Kimono Grab*) with the Parker angles and checks, the technique sequence became difficult, if not impossible, to execute effectively. I was taught to clear the arms straight down and that would bring the head forward so I could chop the throat. But I could also be hit with a head butt. Mr. Parker loved to demonstrate just that at seminars using *Lone Kimono*. If I angled the clear down and in I could cancel the head butt and chop the side of the neck instead. Head butts happen very fast. Angle of Cancellation is a key principle you need to understand and use.

When doing *Dance of Death* I made the common mistake of not keeping my head and upper body in tight. That allowed the opponent to elbow my head, something he was more than happy to demonstrate. I need to be very clear here in stating that Ed Parker never really hurt me in all my contact with him. He hit me hard enough to give me the feel but never made me feel I had to fear him or that he would abuse his position as the teacher. Yes, he knocked the wind out of me. Yes, he stunned me with an elbow sandwich. Yes, he moved me around like a rag doll. These were all things I would vividly remember over the years. He never blew out my knee or knocked out a tooth. I've heard he had done so with some students, I know he knocked out two of my teachers once (they told me the stories), and he told me about breaking a face or two in situations other than street fights (and he paid for some facial reconstruction in those situations as well). He never busted me up.

Other movements were defined that day. When doing *Gift of Destruction* for the handshake I asked him what the difference was between a pull and a jerk. "Jerking is a violent pull", he responded. He was breaking things down as the years passed and made distinctions that he referred to as *measure of degree* in his later writing. You will find mention of nudging, bumping, pulling, jerking, wrenching, etc. which are all useful moves and just have different amounts of energy used depending on the intention.

Timing differences in step-drag and push-drag shuffles were described in "beats". He used the musical term "beat" often. Here he told me the step-drag was one-and-a-half beats while a push-drag was one beat because one foot was in the air, however slightly. I would find many of the high level Kenpo instructors were also good musicians.[5] Mr. Parker played the ukulele and was quite good at it. I think

---

[5] Joe Palanzo played trumpet for the Baltimore Jazz Ensemble, Trejo played the guitar, and Planas played guitar in the Neil Diamond back-up band. Trejo and Planas even cut a CD called Thundering Hammers in the late 90s.

there is some connection between the musical and Kenpo abilities. I was with him and another instructor one day when the other man said he wanted to put the techniques to music to illustrate the cadence each one had. Mr. Parker's response was, "It would just be the sound of a machine gun" and he laughed.

In regard to elbows he said the thumbs should be inward and the shoulders down on horizontal elbows. The thumbs are thus protected and freedom of movement results from relaxing the shoulders. A bit of hunching is fairly common in newer students.

While going through some of the techniques he made points about diverting attention, body fulcrums, and developing power with a knee strike. *Scraping Hoof* illustrates how you divert attention to the hands or upper body so you can work against the lower body. This ties in later in Long Form Three where you learn to combine your lines so that you work the legs then the upper body in the grafted technique combination of *Scraping Hoof* and *Repeated Devastation*. While doing *Crossing Talon* he talked about the body fulcrum used in the ripping claw to the face after the outward elbow to the head and before the inward overhead elbow to the spine. He would later refer to such moves as a burdening check as well, since it kept pressure on the opponent to prevent them from rising as a reaction to the face claw. When executing the right knee strike in *Locked Wing* he emphasized the need to bend the supporting knee. The bent knee aids balance and contributes to power. Straightening the support leg doesn't help much and adversely affects balance.

Seminar

Saturday, November 17

Mr. Parker asked me to come along with him and Jim Mitchell to the Flores Brothers studio in Oxnard, CA. where I met the brothers, Refugio (now deceased) and Jesus Flores. Refugio was the light or bantamweight world kickboxing champ, I believe for the World Karate Association (WKA). Jesus was a top-notch forms competitor who would later make his mark on the national circuit.

In his advanced seminar Mr. Parker talked about depth deception. He taught several combinations as examples and relied on conditioning the opponent's response, a solid principle widely used. He started with using a front hand slap or pat to disturb the opponent's hand and arm, following with a rear hand punch. You did that twice, and then switched to a rear hand slap and then front hand punch.

The first two got the opponent feeling as if you were a one range and the switch-up with the front hand punch actually used the closer weapon, "deceiving him in terms of depth".

He went on to discuss angle deception. This was something he liked a lot and would teach it to many successful tournament fighters. He taught the use of three successive jabs. The first two were straight in, as you would expect. The third would be combined with an angled step up the circle with the rear leg. The step not only brought the punch in at a different angle but allowed more reach, which in turn gave more penetration. It was in these situations he would use the bobbing and slipping we discussed in the basics.

Changing ranges was next and he showed how to go from a punch to medium and short-range weapons. He entered with a blocking punch, striking the arm down and ricocheting up to a vertical punch to the face. Dropping his weight, he'd couple the drop with a horizontal forearm down across the upper chest to bring the opponent's head down a bit. As the head dropped he'd then be a half-beat ahead and extend his arm into a lifting forearm that struck under the chin to snap the head back and hopefully make the opponent bite his tongue. Then he would do a rear crossover forward to facilitate an outward raking back-knuckle across the bridge of the nose and finish that move with an upward outward diagonal elbow to the chin, using a spiral action. He'd get five or six strikes in with a step out and into a rear crossover. It was fast, accurate, and powerful.

He finished up the seminar with further applications of the rear crossover and jabs. The rear crossover enabled him to hit with the rear hand when at the right range, something that normally gets people tied up because they try it at the wrong range. He'd jab with the crossover and then leg sweep with a heel-palm. He threw in some unusual angled punches, too.

He did another seminar at 1pm for beginners and focused on how one move could have many definitions, a subject he would elaborate on often in the next years.

One of his best-remembered presentations there and elsewhere was when he would ask the participants, "What is the meaning of the word light?" He would draw several answers out of them such as light referred to color or complexion, weight, illumination, touch, and even beer (he laughed when he heard that). He wanted them to understand that as one word could have many definitions, so could motion. When they talked about touch he always spoke of Texas karate and would say what they called light touch in

Texas meant you got light on your feet before you hit the ground. Texas fighters had a nationwide reputation of being hard-hitters back then and still may today.

An upward block was what he used to illustrate the concept of one move having more than one definition. The common use of the block is strictly <u>defensive</u>; someone tries to hit your head and you use the upward block to stop them. The <u>offensive defense</u> is what we do in the technique *Lone Kimono*, a defense for a lapel grab. We use the exact same movement but we break the arm with it. (Oops, it got in the way.) <u>Aggressive offense</u> is what we call it when we use the upward block motion as an uppercut to the chin, followed by a forearm to the throat or strike under the jaw. That's found in Long Form Two. One movement; three applications.

He liked to use the cue ball analogy in his teaching, too. He would start by saying that doing Kenpo on an opponent was like shooting pool. "Excuse me, I mean family billiards" he'd say. The group was asked what the main idea of the game was. He'd follow that with stating that the idea was to sink the ball in the pocket and if that was not possible, to position the balls so that the opponent had no opportunity to sink one. He showed how a strike would keep the man busy with his pain and how the checks and position would prevent the opponent from "lining up a shot" on you.

A further analogy to football was used in that he told us you should always have a game plan. Ed Parker was a football player when he was young, had experience with the game strategy, and he used that information in his explanation and execution of Kenpo.

Later that day we also sat on an exam board. I remember Jesus doing a form and he had a different way to do the salutation. Afterward Jim Mitchell, who was there with us, asked him where he had learned it. Jesus told him that he had gotten it from Jim, which surprised him. In later years I would see mutations of things that people would tell me they got from me or someone who got it from me, but after being run through the perception filters it looked much different. It was a lesson in constant review with a qualified instructor to help reduce or prevent that from happening that I would take into the future.

Private lessons

February 1980

"I expect these to be written up and handed back to me", were the instructions I was given early in this lesson. My notes are labeled as General Questions and Answers and dated February 12. The questions were about many different subjects. I've grouped them roughly by subject but they are not in the original order I wrote them down. However, I did mark them as 1) technical-general, 2) technical-specific and, 3) historical/philosophical.

Mr. Parker used to tell seminar groups about the guy who came to him with a roll of toilet paper with questions written on it, his allusion to someone with so many questions they couldn't be done on one sheet of paper. He said that I was that guy. I'm sure there were others and that he probably told them the same thing. But during these lessons he said, "You're asking me things nobody ever asked me."

Technical-general/On stances and maneuvers

When I asked him why we kept our feet pigeon-toed instead of parallel in a horse stance like many systems his answer was this:

"The reason the feet are pigeon-toed in the horse stance is to increase stability due to use of the calf muscles. When the feet are straight ahead there is no support, provided the attack comes from the flank."

This is the same principle he used in a forward bow stance and you can see how he liked it when he used the fighting horse, his favorite stance. This tends to engage the anterior muscle group in the lower leg for support. The comment about the flank refers to the given lines we need to create bracing angles, such as when facing an opponent in a neutral bow.

We talked about cat stances, and he made an interesting observation about the depth and its relationship to what tools to use in response to an attack.

"Close cats are better adapted for side kicks, extended cats for roundhouses. The best cat is the one proportioned for your body."

If you practice kicking using the close cat for a side kick and a roundhouse with the extended cat, you'll get a sense of what he was saying. He qualified it by saying they were all in proportion to your body, going back to the tailoring concept. You don't want your foot out too far. The closer cat requires less time to cock a side kick. We use 45-degree, 90-degree, and reverse cat stances (a high close kneel, actually). This question touched on changes in depth and how it affected your options. It could roughly be equated to changes in proportion in a neutral bow, side horse, and inverted neutral bow. He also stated that barefoot practitioners historically used the cat stance to pick up the vibrations of oncoming horses. In addition, I've asked why a cat is named as such and one of the most interesting answers I got was that it resembled a cat testing the water.

Since I had seen so many versions of hand positions in the cross-outs at the conclusion of a technique I asked him just what the hands and arms should be doing. In my time at the Pasadena school I'd seen everything from tight fists with elbows in to what looked like flailing. I should note that Mr. Parker was not opposed to the occasional theatrical version, arms out in claw position, one forward and down and the other up and back. He'd say you could use it to strike a second opponent as well as cover the first downed man but most of the time he just did it for the effect in a demonstration because it looks dramatic. So what should I do?

"Cross-outs on covers (cover-out) require that the hands be used with the legs and body to protect and counter-balance the action. The cover-out always goes to a corner at a square encompassed by a circle. Thus your opponent may not strike you."

This refers to the Neutral Zone of Defense, which will be described later in another chapter. *"At no time should you go inside the circle. You do your dirty work and get out."* He used an example of a man on his back and pointed out that if he wanted to move his limbs, it was always in a circle. Therefore you should move to the corner because it is not within the circle.

When I listened to the audio recording of this lesson when researching this book I was reminded by a comment I made on the tape that I was taught techniques with a spin cover. Instead of doing a cross out, you spun around in a guard. While it may have an occasional use it doesn't allow you to keep your eyes on the opponent. He would often observe that people would not slide their feet during the cross-out and the loss of contact with the floor as they did so made them look like "dancing chickens". From time to time you'd hear him say to a class, "No dancing chickens."

On breathing

"Breath may be expelled through a technique and regulated to accentuate a strike, or done incrementally. It depends on where you want the emphasis on power. Short, choppy breathing will slow a person down because it's 'one and two and three'. Eliminate the 'ands'. Expel breath from the first to the last hit. Breath encompasses the entire movement."

Like any system, you need to breathe from the diaphragm, down deep. You can let a little out with each move, keeping the amount the same on each. Or you can let more out, and/or more forcefully, on a particular strike.

He used an analogy of a teapot. Turn the heat on and when it boils it whistles due to constriction of the air in the spout. Take the top off the pot and all that energy escapes without the whistle. It's unfocused. He felt that if you compressed and directed it in the manner he described you would hit harder. Short, choppy breathing causes the diaphragm to relax and contract in a manner that does not benefit the practitioner. It's a lot like hyperventilating.

Since body position has such a profound effect on breathing I asked him about the alignment we prefer in Kenpo. My observation was that many karate systems are very straight-backed and kung-fu systems use a more relaxed, almost sunken-chest type of posture. His response was,

"We use a concave chest to keep the diaphragm relaxed before action. Not as collapsed as some Kung-fu styles or as straight-backed as karate. We are between."

The point is made that Kenpo is the happy medium in posture just as it is medium between the hard and soft systems, if you were to classify it. The relaxed posture facilitates movement and allows breathing to happen freely. Some practitioners just carry too much tension in their chests and shoulders. It makes them stiff and less able to react and counter.

Random items

I asked about the egg-shaped perimeter he called the Outer Rim. That was a concept he created to drive home the use of economy of motion because staying inside the egg speeds reaction and countering because it cuts time and distance. This was something that had bugged me for years because he mentioned it in a brief discussion I had with him in 1978, before I became his student. I was at the MARS[6] Nationals in Cleveland, Ohio and he was the center judge

---

[6] Martial Arts Rating System

for black belt forms. I made it a habit to get hints, tips, and criticism from the judges after competition, and I did so this time. I took advantage of the fact that the master of the system had watched me work and I wanted to know what he had to say. Among other things he told me my circles were too big and were "outside the general egg-shaped perimeter". There was no time to get him to elaborate, so I thanked him. When I went back to Illinois I told Mike Sanders about the meeting. Mike really didn't have a clue about the egg-shaped area, and said so. It must have been a fairly recent development on Mr. Parker's part since Mike had studied with Mills Crenshaw and either missed or forgot it, or maybe it wasn't taught. I subsequently misunderstood the egg-shape. There were no references at the time, the *Infinite Insights* books had not been written, we were not IKKA members and had no access to their materials, and there were no videos. My teacher didn't know and it would be another year or so before I got to ask. I thought the egg-shape was lateral instead of vertical, as if standing in a neutral bow and the smaller, tip portion was where your hands were and the larger part of the egg was over your torso. At the time it made sense because he had said I was reaching outside the egg and I thought "He said so, so it must be true." I'm telling you this because so often we think we understand or really don't at all but don't want to let anyone know. Then we build on the misunderstanding and we go astray. It's often more simple and better to find someone and ask, as long as they don't try to hide the fact that they don't know either. Good instructors will say they don't know but know where to find out. That's something I've lived by.

Mike got upset on one point, that being that Mr. Parker had told me my stances were too low. Mike said, "I remember him being in a horse that looked like a rectangle and demanding we do it that way." I worked in a very low stance because I was trying to break into the regional and national rankings and with a predominance of hard-style judges it was working. Later I would bring the stances up to the standard proportions but that was after they had seen me a lot and maybe realized I wouldn't go away.

On another subject, I had seen that many systems' forms had certain moves or sequences in sets of three. Three appears frequently in many things. Our long salutation has a triangle that represents Heaven, Earth, and Man. A triangle is said to be the strongest geometric shape. Look at the Pyramids. What about the Holy Trinity? And the three branches of government we have? Then there is the saying "Three's a crowd". This could go on and on but it ties into the martial arts constantly. There is right, left and center as well as high, middle, and low. As I did some research I found the Chinese systems often did three in a sequence to show internal, external, and combined applications. Ed Parker had a simple reason that serves well, too. *"Techniques repeated three times in forms are for repetition to maintain ability to alternate sides, so odd numbers must be used."* When you look at the forms you tend to see the right and left side and pair those. Mentally you are working with two. If you look at the second half of Long One you see the introduction of threes. If it were simply a matter of working once on the right and once on the left you would only need two moves. Yet that would often leave you in an awkward position. Adding the third repetition brings you back to the first position and that helps you to get to the other lead side more easily. If you go back and play with sections of forms that have three repetitions and take the third one out you will find yourself on the odd side, normally having to start with your left, the weak side for most of us. Maybe it was an odd question but it opened some doors for me.

Technical-specific/center-line theory

It's generally accepted that the center-line runs down the center of your body from the top of your head down, when viewed from the front. It's called the sagittal plane. Many of the vital targets lie along that line. Don't forget that it runs down the back as well and the spine is a great reference line and target. There is a lateral center-line that runs from the top of your head down through your ears and shoulders and below, too. It's called the coronal plane. The one dividing upper body from lower is the axial plane.

"Center-line striking is more powerful because you get the proper body alignment and your back-up mass is behind your action."

But how do you get there? Is it from the outside in or the inside out? Shouldn't your punch go from point of origin to the target?

"Your center-line is not from outside in, but is formed when you follow the circle or your ribs and punch from there, the inside."

Ed Parker used his body in what I describe as a turret method. By following your ribs with your elbow, no matter which way you turn, you can strike with the center-line aligned.

One of Mr. Parker's first black belts was John McSweeney. John was known as the "Father of Irish Karate" for having brought Kenpo there when he went to Trinity College in Dublin. In his later years in Chicago, John was known as the leading proponent of a handgun shooting method called point-shooting. The method largely depends on keeping your elbow in close to your center-line and rotating the body with it in that turret-like method Ed Parker used. John's method was quite fast, deadly accurate, and became widely accepted. I like to think Mr. Parker's thinking on elbow usage contributed to it. John eventually moved to Florida and settled in Ft. Myers, not far from my school. We spent many hours there in the sunshine, reminiscing about our teacher and discussing other subjects. What's not to like about an Irish storyteller?

Elbow strikes

Kenpo is a close range system, so it stands to reason that we use lots of elbows. Mr. Parker had some interesting uses of elbow techniques but the following questions were about the basic principles. If you watch people throw their elbows you'll often see that the elbow moves upward first and then follows a circle to the target. It's a lot like the way many people throw a roundhouse (wheel) kick. Mr. Parker didn't do that, and he didn't like seeing it either. Going up when it is needed to go forward loses energy. Then, as he described it, you have to put the brakes on to get the strike or kick going forward in the direction it needs to go. Overall it loses a lot of momentum. His method was to keep it in tight and throw the elbow much like a punch. It provides margin for error and increases power.

"Elbow strikes rotate from palm-up to palm-down for torque. The bicep and upper forearm muscles pinch together for striking mass."

This description illustrates what he thought about body momentum, compact unit, and delivery. Too many practitioners work their elbows without the compact unit being used and others get stuck because they try to keep the elbow locked in place. That's what he meant by "brakes". It makes the elbow more like a push, just as if you tensed a punch prematurely. Timing is the real issue here.

"There are solid, head-on strikes and ricochets (glances). The Parker system teaches the application of both head-on and glancing elbows, along with sandwiches and forearm strikes. The examples in the techniques account for the reaction to previous strikes and then what is available for follow-up." I asked him about when we use a circle to deliver an elbow as opposed to when to use a

ratchet. I don't think he was using the term "ratchet" yet then because my notes say, "collapsing". Ratchet is a better term. He stated, *"Collapses (ratchets) use a shuffle to make up for power loss. A circle may be used when there is time."*

We discussed the technique called *Snapping Twig* as an example. The third move is a right inward raking back-knuckle to the bridge of the nose. A right inward elbow sandwich, normally with a shuffle, follows it. He did it on me and showed the timing changes. He said that if you had time you followed the circle you started with the rake and delivered the sandwich. If the man were dropping down or back the ratchet would be faster. The general rule in Kenpo is that shuffles go where they are needed and another rule is that you usually shuffle when you go to the shorter weapon. At about the time I learned (re-learned, actually) this technique there was considerable discussion about the shuffles. Apparently there had just been a change disseminated. The "original" technique had one shuffle, and that was with the elbow. Another was added in the second move, with a left thrusting chop to the throat. The troops were upset, as people get in this sort of situation, that something had changed. People generally don't like change and change raises questions. I believe that's unavoidable, no matter how good your communication system is.

However, the change prevailed over time. It was a good change, adding reach and power to the technique. If nothing else, Ed Parker had a good reason for doing anything he did.

Talking about rakes in this technique brought out this observation, *"There is no difference between a slice and a rake. A slice uses one portion of a natural weapon in contact. Multiple slices become a rake, like a corrugation."* It's interesting that he would state there is no difference, then go on to define the difference. He also mentioned that a snap is the result of a whip. In later lessons he would say it was the magnitude that differentiated a snap and a whip. It's just nomenclature.

Historical/philosophical/protocol

A black belt of mine named Bill Roma commented regarding the ongoing question about whether it's Kenpo or Kempo; "No wonder other systems make fun of us. We can't even decide if it's an "n" or an "m" in our name." So I asked.

"Kenpo with an "n" has been spelled that way since before karate became popular. Much of this is probably due to dialectic differences. Most Okinawan styles called it "Karate Kenpo". Karate was a style of Kenpo. Today

karate is the popular term. Kenpo Karate denotes our system and is recognized as such."

This was one-and-a-half years before his first volume of *Infinite Insights* was published. In that book he included a history and these elements are discussed, so I defer to and direct you to it. We got into what historians say and in context to the "n and m" discussion he said, "When a punch hits you it still hurts. It's still a punch no matter what language."

The difference between style and system came up in conversation. He said, "The system is the method, and style is the application (execution) of the method". He would often illustrate the idea by asking a class what three famous painters had in common and would use such artists as Picasso, Van Gogh, and Rembrandt as examples. The answer, he would explain, was "They use canvas, paint, and a brush." By this time the class was visualizing three canvasses as he would mime the actions of a painter as he told them that while the materials in use were the same (the system), the way they used them was quite different (the style). He added that they also created illusions of height, width, and depth. It was in this context that he would talk about how you could take ten of his black belts to demonstrate the same technique and they'd all do it differently although they would also all be correct. His tailoring principle was highlighted in this manner along with his emphasis that one needed to know and apply the principles in order to be consistent with the rules of Kenpo. It was at this time he said to me, "It is my system." In later years he would say, "It is our system" and explained that it belonged to us all.

When I asked him about certain protocols to be followed in the studio he said that Chinese term, *Sifu,* would be the proper term for an instructor in our system, as opposed to the Japanese term, S*ensei.* His remark was, "I would rather be called a Sifu than a Sensei". Much of the traditional Chinese terminology and lyrical names for techniques had been eliminated from the system as it evolved and I think this is where the English forms of respectful address such as Mr., Mrs., and Miss became predominant. It was nearly always "Mr. Parker" although you'd hear "Sifu Parker" occasionally and maybe a hard-stylist would call him "Sensei Parker". Today the English terms are used, although the late seniors Tom Kelly and Steven LaBounty still use the Chinese terms of Si-bok (senior instructor) and Si-gung (teacher's teacher) respectively, and are typically addressed as such by junior practitioners.

The Chinese term for a school is *kwoon* and he said that would be the technically correct term for a Kenpo school. However, he referred to our schools as "studios". When I asked why he said, "Because it is a place of work or creation."

When speaking of seniority, what is the proper way to line up when in class? I'd seen at least two ways to do it when keeping the seniors students in the front. I'm not considering the random line-ups you may see at a seminar, or the variations that place the newer students in front. Most Kenpo schools I'd been to place the highest rank at the right front corner of the mat, to my left as I faced the class. A few were notable in that it was the opposite, with the seniors on my right. Which was the preferred way?

He said the first configuration was correct for the following reason. *"When you turn around, as in a demo, your highest ranking student is on your right, your strong side"*, he told me.

As a side note, in traditional Chinese schools, the teacher always has his back to the wall, which is normally where the school's logo or crest is. Another reason is that it is believed that if you teach with your back to the students they can steal your *chi*. That's because the kidneys are the magnets that draw in chi and they are now exposed to the students, who can draw off your energy. Interesting.

There is logic to the class being lined up with the higher ranks on the right when facing them because they would be on your symbolic strong side, but not if you turn around to show a united front to an audience. Ed Parker was big on that aspect, being the head of the IKKA and having a standard uniform regulation, etc. He said his line-up showed respect for a higher authority, especially when facing the flag. He said "the" flag, not "a" flag. Ed Parker did not like people bowing to foreign flags, as so many schools teach. Look at page 15 of *Memories of Ed Parker*, where you see a group shot including him and Professor Chow with a large American flag in the background. He respected our flag and realized that others training in Kenpo abroad would respect their own flag. He never dictated that an American flag be placed in a Kenpo classroom.

When there is more than one instructor at the front of the class or at an exam, they line up facing the group with the senior instructor in front, just forward of the rest. The next senior is to the right, the next senior to the left, then next to the right, and so on. This shows continuity with the class line-up and is why I use both methods.

I asked him about age limits to get a black belt. This may seem a strange question today given that most schools issue black belts to children on a regular basis. In fact, there's an unwritten competition to see who can produce the youngest one. You'll see a four-year-old black belt on television once in a while. Back in our systems' history nobody below the age of 16 was tested for black. Mr. Parker felt it was necessary due to maturity and used the issuance of a driver's license as a benchmark. The first 16 year-old black belt he promoted was Casey Clayton of Salt Lake City. I met Casey back in the late 70s when he came to Chicago to visit Mike Sanders. They had both trained in the Salt Lake City school with Mills Crenshaw. Casey later went to Grass Mountain, Taiwan to train in traditional arts and came back to the U.S. to found a school in Salt Lake City called the House of the Night Wind, where he taught both Chinese arts and Kenpo. I have to say that one of my young students, Tony Velada, broke the mold by being tested and promoted to black at age 14 by Mr. Parker and myself in Chicago in the late 80's.

Mr. Parker thought children should be taught the system with modified weapons and targets. They should be taught the principles so that they, too, could become self-correcting, just as he wished the adults to be. As they got older and continued their training they could go through the system again, learn the adult versions, and review the principles. Many of them did just that and they are teaching today.

Finally, I asked him about the formal salutation. The first part is in his book, *Secrets of Chinese Karate*. In there he gives a skeletal description of what the movements <u>mean</u>. In *Infinite Insights into Kenpo, Vol.1* and *Vol. 5,* he describes what the movements <u>are</u>, that is, how to do them. He told me the salutation was his creation, being a combination of old and new salutes blended just as his system was a combination of old and new, what he called "Modern Day Kenpo". The first part was from the old Shaolin salute, and the second has elements shared with many karate systems of the last century plus his movements, thus the old and new. His description to me is as follows.

"The salutation comes naturally from the shoulder with the right crossover to a cat. 'I cover my treasure and humbly perform before you and hope you enjoy what I do. Accept it for what it is.' Then step back to indicate there is no challenge to anyone in the audience. The old meaning was 'The scholar and martial artist are going forward, fighting back-to-back, and pulling our country together

again'." He added that there were several self-defense techniques in the salutation. Here he stated that there is a difference between a challenge salute and a demonstration salute, something Mike Sanders had told me. The demonstration salute steps back with the second step to the point of origin. The challenge salute does not, ending one step forward of the point of origin. It is used when you think you're better than anyone in the audience and you're ready to fight to prove it. I've seen it done intentionally once to a group, and either nobody caught it or thought it was worth acting on. I questioned it and the instructor who did it said it was intentional and he wanted to see if anyone caught it.

The instructions for the second half were to step out to the left into a horse with open hands high in a triangle, *"I am friendly and unarmed".* The hand over fist followed with *"I do not wish to use my weapons"* and then the prayer position with *"I pray, since you have forced me, for forgiveness that I must be a barbarian to handle the situation."* He added as an aside to me, *"That I have to be an animal",* which accounts for the claws on the close.

Additionally, he emphasized that the hands descended in height and came inward in depth when looked at from the open hands to shielded hand to the prayer position. The fact that the left foot stepped out and later is brought in at the end signified the weaker becoming stronger. We know the left foot moves out to show casting off weakness and that training makes us stronger. I've found in my travels that many people know how to do the salutation but don't know what it means, or maybe just know pieces. I think it's important that a history lesson be given when the salutation is taught.

The next days were review of the orange and purple belt material. He asked me to give him a ride to the airport the next day since he was leaving out of Los Angeles International and the ride would give us a chance to talk some more. I was more than happy to do this and looked forward to it.

We discussed master key movements, which he defined as a move that could be used in four to five situations. He used the technique, *Scraping Hoof,* a defense against a full-nelson as an example. He said it could be used also for bear hugs, etc. I use it today in women's self-defense classes for that reason. It works for a full-nelson, bear-hug free, bear-hug pinned, forearm choke, yoke grab, or even a hammerlock attempt.

My notes say we talked about the use of the technique manuals. He said they were geared for beginners and indicated the best hand and foot positions for them at their level. Alterations could be made later with expansion of knowledge. I interpret this today to be his answer at the time because this does not account for the advanced material being in the *Accumulative Journal*. They're not beginners except in one respect and that is that they just began their advanced training. The seniors in the system who were there when the manual was created say that it was done for the Ed Parker Karate Studio franchises. The franchise owner would have the book, which would be the template, for what was to be taught. Legally, a franchise requires a standard operating procedures manual. Huk Planas said it was he and Tom Kelly who helped Ed Parker standardize the techniques and manuals that became the *Accumulative Journal* and when Mr. Parker realized he could make some money on it he started to sell it to the IKKA general membership. Huk later told me Mr. Parker and Tom Kelly wrote the material and that he was the test subject to see if he did what they intended when they read the manual aloud to him. It has gone through at least four versions, with many others being variations on the theme.

I asked him about the rear hand positions used in such techniques as *Dance of Death* and *Flashing Mace*. These were unfamiliar to me since they weren't taught by either of my first instructors. He said the rear hand could be dangled or raised respectively to simulate certain conditions that may be encountered on the street and familiarize you with the mechanics of defending from these positions.

One thing I remember about this ride was that it was my first time seeing one of the mudslides that are so well known in Southern California. We came up on a delay that was caused by one and was just finishing being cleared. He was a bit concerned about being late for his plane. He told me a story about being rushed to make his plane and was approached by a man who wanted to sell him a book. This was common in the 70s and early 80s when airport security was not as it is today and anyone could pretty much go anywhere in an airport. Members of the Hare Krishna sect went to the airports to fund their activities by selling books to airline passengers. They wore the orange robes of an Oriental monk and shaved their heads, leaving only a ponytail. Most people considered them to be a nuisance. He described how he was running to make his plane when the man in street clothes with a book to sell got in his way and wouldn't move. He heel-palmed him in the chest hard and got a surprise, he'd hit him hard enough to knock a wig off and exposed the ponytail. He laughed when he told the story and said they had become such a bother that they had taken to disguising themselves. He didn't know the man was one of them but obviously took some satisfaction in unmasking him.

I had to laugh when I heard myself on these lesson tapes saying the same thing I'd heard from students so many times over the years, that being, "I'm having a hard time with the terminology." His response was, "That's what you're asking for", by asking questions to help understand the system. Ed Parker did not suffer a fool very well. He could tell if you were genuinely asking or just talking to hear yourself talk. I was with him when he was auditioning a man to demonstrate at the Internationals one year. This person said he represented Bruce Lee's Jeet Kune Do (JKD). Mr. Parker and I sat out on his back lanai and he asked him what he wanted to do for his demo. He said he would do some rope skipping, focus pad work, kick a shield, do some *chi sao* and some sparring. Mr. Parker was not impressed. After all, Ed Parker introduced Bruce Lee to the world and had spent much time with him discussing philosophy and combat principles. It was Ed Parker who introduced Dan Inosanto to Bruce Lee, and Dan would take JKD into the future. The fact that this man had managed to get some of Ed Parker's time and the chance at getting exposure on the stage at one of the world's largest and prestigious karate tournaments really meant something. Instead of having something to showcase the system he practiced he wanted to show how well he could skip rope and how hard he could punch. Mr. Parker didn't sit long for this and asked him some questions. Our guy proceeded to tell Mr. Parker what Bruce had in mind with his system and philosophies. That got a rise out of the Kenpo master. He exploded, "Oh really? Were you there? I was, and that certainly wasn't what Bruce had in mind when we talked about it." My input was not asked for or needed. This man was escorted to the door. What a privilege to be with Ed Parker at times like this. Not just on a classroom floor or in a private lesson, but when he interacted with people outside the system and in other situations I would be there for in the future. Such opportunities gave me insight into how he thought and that, I believe, helped me tremendously to understand what he was teaching.

A pattern emerged in which I would travel to Pasadena about every three months and stay a week. The seminars to follow would have Ed Parker visit my studio twice a year.

First Chicago Seminar

Summer 1980

I sponsored Ed Parker's first-ever seminar in Chicago. One of my students told me that he was informing someone from another system that his instructor trained with Ed Parker and that the man didn't believe him, saying that Parker didn't have any students in Chicago. About 125 people who did believe it showed up for the event. They came out of the woodwork. Some of them just wanted to see him teach and shake his hand because they'd heard so much about him. Chicago hadn't been on his travel list very often. I know he'd been there in 1963 when the World Karate Federation (WKF) held the first big karate tournament in the U.S. there. That may well have been the last time until that summer of 1980.

He taught his Advanced Karate Theories seminar, speaking of his ideas on the phonetics of motion, point of origin, the rearrangement principle and much more, all items he would reiterate again and again over the years everywhere. He answered many questions and worked the class out.

I distinctly remember him demonstrating the rearrangement principle on me and just clipping my jaw with an elbow sandwich. The bell went off in my head, my hands dropped, and I rocked back on my heels but didn't lose it. I'd never been hit like that before and it wasn't a full-on shot, just a glancing blow. I've got the pictures; see one below.

Prior to this event there had been a battle of words raging in the karate magazines about the Parker system with one particularly vocal opponent writing in about how nonsensical the slapping was in the Parker system. Comments were made about how we slap ourselves to death (to which he said, "If we slap ourselves to death just think what we do to an opponent.") in our techniques. As fate would have it the subject arose at the seminar and he explained how it was used as a timing device for teaching and as a check or back-up parry or block. And it happened that the same man who was so vocal in the magazine was there in the seminar. He approached Mr. Parker afterward, explained who he was, and apologized, saying he was ignorant and now understood. This same sort of thing happened a few years later with another instructor from a hard-style who came into my school and introduced himself. He was not a critic of the system but truly wanted to understand why we did some of the things we did. I invited him into the next seminar as my guest. It was there that he became "enlightened" as to the potency of the back-knuckle strike. He believed that the strike didn't have much power and Mr. Parker changed his mind without even laying a hand on him. His next Letter to the Editor was printed and it contained praise for the back-knuckle, thanks to Ed Parker.

We had a test and that was when I produced my first two black belts under the Parker line, Joe Merritt and Brian Fox. I had two other black belts, Jon Landin and Ed Maul, who were black belts already but their names didn't make it to the family tree he would publish in *Infinite Insights into Kenpo, Vol. 1*. He asked me for the names twice, I submitted them both times and only the two made it. He told me he lost them. I only mention this because if it happened to them it could have happened to others, so don't discount certain claims that someone should have been on the tree. Others who assisted at the exam are still training and teaching today, almost 30 years later. They are Jon Landin, Kurt Barnhart, Manuel Rivera, and Ed Bilski. They would be instrumental in my being able to work toward my goals and I dedicate this book to them. As of 2023 they are all still active.

Private lessons

June 16 - 21, 1980

Once again my notes are labeled as General Question and Answer. There are 14 categories I asked him about and much of it was to get a definition from him. The resources a Kenpo student has today were mostly non-existent then. As I mentioned earlier, there was no *Infinite Insights* series yet, with their glossaries in the back. *The Encyclopedia of Kenpo* likely wasn't even considered yet since he was planning to have the *Insights* book as the main reference. Remember, it was to be one book, not five volumes.

I had my list of questions and sat down to ask them. There's a saying that when you ask a question you really already know the answer. I found this to often be true when talking with him. I'd ask a question, in the course of it realize the answer and really just get it verified by him. Maybe it was the "pressure" of being there with him, one on one in the presence of the master, that made me think just a bit harder. I hate to waste people's time and I sure didn't want to waste his. On the plus side he told me, "I like to rap with you". I guess I asked some good questions and was able to contribute to what he was doing in some way.

Zone theory, again

He'd been working out his explanations and refining his presentations of zone theory. The rudiments of it were published in *Secrets of Chinese Karate* in 1963 and it would become even more developed by 1986 when he produced the fourth volume of *Infinite Insights*. In the meantime he was hammering it into his students, those of us spread around the country representing him, and at seminars.

The thinking behind the development of his representations of the zones is what is really interesting. One of the first times I asked him about why we had four vertical zones instead of two or three he said it was because that was just the way it looked to him. But in this lesson he said they were "developed from looking at an individual's defense." He believed the quartering of the body helped to develop more control over the opponent's zones. His thinking with the horizontal zones was pretty simple, too. You have to stand on one leg, so that leaves you with three free limbs to work with. If you put one in each zone, you're covered. One hand covers the high zone, the other the middle zone, and one leg covers the low zone. He was funny in that he wished he had more hands and lamented he only had four limbs. I could imagine Ed Parker as one of those multi-armed gods of war. That would be a problem because when he worked on you it felt like he had more than two hands, anyway.

His view of a person's body was that the zones opened and closed like Venetian blinds. If you pulled down and across the body it closed the vertical and height zones. If you let him rotate forward to punch, they opened. And if you pulled too much across, the ones in the back would open so the opponent could spin with an attack. So dividing the areas up into smaller chunks and considering how their defense was set up would offer the control he wanted. Height zones essentially worked the same way. Today when I teach the beginner basics of how to form the neutral bow I make sure to cover the position of the limbs in relation to the zones. In addition, I try to make sure that the neutral bow as taught is a reference position and that the limbs may have to change position depending on what the range and positions are, among other factors.

He described the depth zones as being viewed from a profile, and discussed the Outer Rim, too. Again I refer you to his books and offer the material here as an attempt to give you insight into his thought process.

Greatest hits

"What's the fastest weapon to throw?" I asked. His immediate response was that it was the front-leg side kick. He said it was like a jab to the knee. *"The easiest area to damage is the shin, using this kick. There is basically no defense for a low attack there."* He shows that relationship in the second section of Long Form Two when we do the snapping side kick and simultaneous vertical jab. He liked it, especially when you were wearing shoes and could do more damage with the edge of the sole. About the only thing you can do as a defense is move your leg. If he was jabbing or striking at your eyes you might have trouble getting that leg out of the way, too. *"A kick is technically a strike",* he'd say.

Kenpo is known for the open-hand and finger strikes. I remember people back in the 70s cringing and saying, "You guys poke people in the eyes." At this time Mr. Parker told me that finger techniques should be for advanced levels, however, an introduction was necessary. For beginners the fingers should be closer for support and no one finger should lead another. Of course, advanced techniques don't always follow these guidelines but they are good for beginners.

Back to the future

Many of the terminology questions I asked at this time were later to be included in the *Infinite Insights* books. The original *Accumulative Journal* had terminology sheets included with your technique manuals, broken down by rank. They only went up to Green belt. The following definitions were not in the manual and most were not in the glossaries of the *Infinite Insights* books, although some were described in detail in certain chapters. They may not "match" the definitions in later books, either, but also may contain information that was not included in those publications. You may even find them easier to understand in this early form.

- Jamming – is a form of pinning. It uses more force in the movement just as jerking is a violent form of pulling.
- Hugging – The difference between hugging and pinning is that more body surface is in contact, like in a bear hug.
- Spinning and twirling – Spinning is a rotating movement while in contact with the ground. Twirling is basically the same move while airborne.

- Shuffles – are basically pushing or pulling actions. What you plan to do and the intended target will determine which shuffle to use.
- Cover Outs – Covers are essential because without them one remains within his (the opponent's) critical range. Double covers prevent his using one crossover to get to you.

Other ideas were included in this lesson. These are not definitions but explanations of a particular aspect of something.

- Blocking – A pinning block pins the opponent's weapon, generally against his own body. Walls, floors, etc may also be used. The opponent need make no motion for you to apply this action.
- Checking – You must always place your hands in the area of the most weapons, in terms of those weapons being available to counter you. (He really liked to use the phrase, "In terms of".) Later I'd be taught there was a difference between checking and covering. This definition fits the later description of covering or a position check. Words such as "hinder" and "restrain" would be used in checking definitions later.

- Reacting and countering – There is a definite difference in reacting and countering. Reacting is your response, for example, a novice might block. The counter is the follow-up attack. Advanced students may eliminate the block, combining an evasive move with their counter simultaneously.
- Stance – self-defense techniques are taught initially from a standing, feet-together position. This is done to familiarize the student with moving from an awkward position. Starting from a neutral bow is taught later to work the student from this now comfortable position.

I have done a lot of thinking about this over the years. I agree that the feet-together position may be awkward in that you are pretty exposed. The system also teaches you to react from many other positions and this is only a start. See page 220 in *Lee Wedlake's Kenpo Companion* for a more in-depth explanation. You get standard techniques taught from a standard-type neutral bow and from a neutral with the hands reversed (rear hand high and front hand low). You work from the ground and from a kneeling position. Those positions keep you covered. While the standing position may be more open, it also allows you to use any one of your four weapons and to move to any direction, under certain circumstances. The main element is that you must not be planted, flat-footed with a 50/50 weight distribution. You have to shift back and forth from one leg to another to pull this off. And that's why you shouldn't really stand (meaning, be stationary) in a neutral, you should be moving. It's just a thought.

In this lesson I learned a fascinating bit of Parker psychology. He had taken some time to develop names for the techniques and part of that was because he wanted to get away from some of the Chinese terminology inherent in the system. Since it is an American system the names should be in English and use an English equivalent. "Spinning hook kick", or some such replaced "The Dragon whips tail". But here he told me, *"The names were given to add incentive to the learning process as well as to aid in the retention of the sequences."* A name was to give a mental hook, to invoke a mental image that would spark the memory. The code names helped. He said the student would read the list of techniques and speculate on what the techniques were. *"I would teach him Triggered Salute and then tell him that next lesson we would do Dance of Death. It generated curiosity and excitement, and would have him looking forward to the next class."* Since what we do is intangible, Ed Parker made it tangible by printing a list that each student could have. It was that thinking that was expanded on with the creation of the *Accumulative Journal.*

Private lessons

November 1980

This lesson was spent mostly on teaching and training methods. I believe there are a lot of crossover instructors from other arts teaching Kenpo who never actually had systematic training in our system. What they got was from either spotty private lessons, seminars or in today's world, the Internet. This resulted in them being able to teach the techniques and forms but lacking in the day-to-day classroom drill portion of the course, and often some other crucial elements. I've seen video in which a fairly well-known East Coast instructor stated he didn't know the application but this was his best guess.

"Relate angles and execution on simple technique to application, then add posture." He used the Star Block as an example. You learn it in a horse but you could then add switches, step-throughs, shuffles, etc. I tell people today that *Lone Kimono* is really just the first three moves of the Star Block.

"The forms should be done more than one way to impart ideas on the various aspects of the techniques involved." I explain this in my books on the forms and he did it in the *Infinite Insights* books. He wrote that you should practice in confined areas, on a slope, in sand, and so on. This is all good advice. Practice with timing and weapon changes, actual opponents, facing different directions, etc.

"In self-defense training, attack and defense should be practiced from various stances such as natural, neutral bows, to feel the various strengths of movements and maneuvers involved." Do *Five Swords* from both neutral bows, on your knees or on your back. This is an eye-opener.

The tendency for some people to lean over too much while striking in a reverse bow triggered a question about how much lean was too much. We know it when we see it but what's the guiding rule?

"When moving in opposite directions, at a certain point the actions cancel each other and power is diminished." You can see how the action of leaning too much forward and away would detract from the power of a hammerfist in a reverse bow. The upper body leaning out would take away the weight needed from the strike or leg buckle. The method he used when doing this actually dropped weight in

and/or down with the strike, depending on if you were shuffling in or rotating into the reverse bow.

Flow was discussed as a part of this conversation. He said, *"Action from action is the hardest to counter. Make movement flow with no wasted action."* This is a cornerstone in Kenpo. For example, when defending against a gun it's a good idea to start your technique when the gunman says, "Get your hands up!" because he expects to see your hands move. If you were to raise your hands, hesitate or stop, then begin a defense you would give him more opportunity to counter you. He used to illustrate this point with a story about two karate fighters in a ring. Traditional fighters will often stand completely still then suddenly explode with an attack. Often the attacker is expertly countered and people would say in awe, "He read his mind." "No," Mr. Parker countered, "He was motionless and then he moved, which made his intentions easier to read. Action from action is hardest to counter." It is an interesting contrast that in many Eastern arts the practitioner stands very still and then attacks, while many Western arts are constantly moving and flow into an attack.

Private lessons

March 1981

Most of these lessons were dedicated to performance of specific techniques and forms. I recorded my lessons on cassette tape.

"Kenpo offers explosive action with minimum target exposure". This is one characteristic he admired so much in Professor Chow, the fact that he was so powerful, explosive, and slipped in with minimum exposure. The checks that Ed Parker inserted into his brand of Kenpo enhanced this facet even more. If you look back at his first book, *Kenpo Karate - Law of the Fist and Empty Hand*, you see that he looked almost like a hard-stylist. He used a forward leaning stance and chambered his hands at his hips most of the time. As he matured as a martial artist he employed the use of checks and this allowed him even greater protection, something he passed along to us. Now you have to ask the question, "Where did the checks come from?"

There is speculation that he took them from the Filipino arts. Possibly, but boxers "check", and so do Indonesian and other Chinese arts. He told the following story of when and where he was that he realized the importance of the check. It doesn't answer where they came from but it does address why they were incorporated.

When he was a young man in college in Utah he would go hunting with a friend. On one occasion his friend shot a deer and knocked it down. They both approached it and his friend bent down to inspect the animal, thinking it was dead. At that moment the animal gave a final kick and its hoof struck his friend in the throat, killing him. He realized that even in death the ability to retaliate still existed. He told this story in many seminars and attributed it as the impetus to add checks to the system.[7] His first book, *Kenpo Karate, Law of the Fist and Empty Hand* and printed in 1960 shows no checks in the techniques. By 1970 the checks were formally in the system with the publication of the *Accumulative Journal*.

---

[7] He told this story in the October 1984 seminar in Chicago.

Chicago seminars

April 12, 1981

I scheduled two seminars for him, one beginner and one advanced. Joe Palanzo, from Baltimore, who would later become one of the systems' 10th degrees, was there. Mr. Parker was in a great mood and had the guys laughing. The participants were a very mixed group. There were people there in street clothes and Tang Soo Do uniforms, Filipino stylists and a variety of Kenpo people. One thing I always did when I'd have him out was discuss the subjects and publish them ahead of time whenever possible. That said, Ed Parker taught many elements of these seminars on points that he and I thought would be helpful to everyone involved. He would cover subjects that I had become more familiar with in previous lessons and would be going into more depth on in the next few months. About a year before we had gotten into the zone theories and he really emphasized them here. He stressed that we should examine target areas in all positions versus looking at the standard targets of a man standing vertically. How zones opened and closed was examined using grabs to create angles of cancellation. He described the concept of the "traveling eye", an idea he used to describe how your weapons should be able to see targets. "Use your imagination and visualize what your weapons see", he said. He'd tell you to put eyes in your foot, looking up, to see what targets were available. His commentary on this included a statement that "Lack of knowledge may cause you to back out and re-await an opening." He stressed that it was important to train in such a manner so that you could work from any position.

After describing the standard height, width, and depth zones he went into the obscure zone, using an analogy to a motorcycle cop. "What do they do?" he asked, "They get in your blind spot." He wanted you to use the obscure zone. In many seminars I heard him say your shot should come from where it was unseen, so that the man "would swear a midget hit him."

As he demonstrated how he worked his way through the zones he talked about how people have a tendency to go for the head too much. His analogy to a meal was used and he said "I like to think of myself as an enzyme" and indicated a progressive chewing motion with his hand. As I mention elsewhere in this book, he loved to eat. He would say that Polynesians would only stop eating when their jaws got tired from chewing. With his appetizer, soup, salad, main course and dessert analogy of an opponent to being a meal, he said that many go straight for the main dish too often. This was coupled with his minor/major principles and illustrated that pain occupies the mind. "If you have a toothache and you come before me, I can show you how I can make you forget it". His point obviously was that his damage to your weapons and guard would engage your mind and allow him to get to the main course easier. Furthering the meal analogy I've been told he used to say, "My knuckles are carnivorous and they hunger for human flesh."[8]

Part of this first seminar was dedicated to use of knives and sticks. Many of the points he made this day are described in the next section on my private lessons in California the next month.

Using the up-side of a circle to cut was something he favored because he believed it was helped by borrowed force. He had the group do some footwork patterns and added knife work to them to reinforce the idea. His method allowed you to cut four times in two moves and he followed

---

[8] Related by Joe Palanzo.

that with, "How can he squawk that he didn't get his money's worth?"

He told of two nephews who brought one of Los Angeles' best Mexican knife fighters to see him. When he saw the man used a linoleum knife sharpened on both sides, he felt the man knew what he was doing. They decided to play. The man put his left arm up horizontally and held the knife in his right. The left could be wrapped in a coat if needed. "What's wrong with this?" he asked the seminar group. It allowed him to check him off, was his answer, re-emphasizing what he covered in the first part of the seminar. He told the class the move he had just taught them was what he successfully did to the Mexican.

Ed Parker developed knife concepts such as filleting, tenderizing, reaming, slicing, and thrusting; preferably using a double–edged knife, but today used a Parker knife to demonstrate. During the seminar he kept using the Parker knife to get his ideas across and used the sheath as a substitute knife, a tactic he often used in teaching.

That certain things could be done with a club that couldn't be done with a knife, such as switching hands was a major point. Of course, you <u>can</u> switch hands but you have to be careful that you don't grab the blade or drop it.

Much of the rest of the class was taken up with his teaching many of the principles that are commonly taught today but weren't back then. His phonetics of motion, the use of sharp and flat weapons, elimination of reverse motion, and opposite/reverse presentations were made. Yet there are a few more statements he made that are well worth time to re-visit.

He discussed the elements of power. I do mean discussed, since he had the audience participating. He listed the components as being velocity, emotion, balance, timing, energy, torque, alignment, marriage of gravity, penetration, and breathing, among others. Having the air in you already was pointed out as being key. Relaying the rotation from the foot to the hip to the shoulder and arm is paramount. Use the kinetic chain.

One should exhaustively examine positions in a technique from both your perspective and the opponent's before going on to that of the spectator. And when you do, "You get diarrhea of the mind. I guarantee it", he said.

This seminar was loaded with well-known Parker stories, comments, and analogy. Like any other well-seasoned speaker he had a memorized presentation but he was flexible with it just as he was with his martial art. Of the motions he said, "You have to learn the motions well enough to become extemporaneous." And of the principles he said, "Your own past experiences are the same as what we employ in the martial arts. When you see the relationships of what you have in music, writing, and speech, it's all the same."

He also told the story about an altercation with multiple opponents he had along a freeway when his pregnant wife, Leilani, was with him. You'll find it in the back of the book in the section with stories and analogies and labeled "The slow-motion cigarette".

The second seminar, for beginners, was opened with a challenge. He asked the class to imagine a pencil he had in his hand was a cigarette, described which end was lit and which was filtered, and if they would tell him how to smoke it. Someone said, "Put it in your mouth", at which time he placed it in his mouth sideways. "No, no", they said, "Put the end in your mouth". He put the "lit" end in his mouth. Then he took it out and admonished the class to be precise in their descriptions of motion. By analyzing what you are doing precisely you can understand the principles, and if you understand principles you can be self-correcting. This was a major goal of his, to get us to understand the principles and be able to correct our own mistakes. In my years as an instructor in other disciplines, only one trainer I had used an analogy like Ed Parker's to get the point across.

This seminar included much of the same material I had been introduced to back in 1979 at the Oxnard seminar. Today he would use *Lone Kimono* to present his ideas on multiple definitions of motion, *Parting Wings* to illustrate compounding movements, *Crashing Wings* and *Leaping Crane* to reinforce zone theory, checking, and using pain to occupy the mind. He also used the term "Polynesian paralysis" to get the people to understand that you can get the opponent to come to you in such a fashion that you can use borrowed force to enhance your blows, all the while saying he was too lazy to go to the opponent so he had to get the opponent to come to him. He talked about "jet lag", an everyday term we're all familiar with but that he used to get one to think about not leaving part of your body behind where it could be hit.

He then asked the class to work on the left side of techniques, telling them that the effort they put into re-analyzing what they had done on the first side in order to learn the second was a big help in understanding.

While he taught them the *Lone Kimono* technique and spoke of Polynesian paralysis, he added a hammerfist and a cover-out to the base to show that anything could be added to. As he did the hammerfist to the groin we heard, "If he's wearing a cup I want the shrapnel to kill him." While demonstrating it with a reverse bow shift he showed why the Kenpo stylist disdains the words "and" and "but" in context to technique execution. "And" movements slowed you down because they acted like an "and then" timing, he believed. The "but" was really "butt" because it referred to bad body alignment in which the hips jut out, causing the opponent's body to be bumped back, away from your strike. With the cover out he told them the distance it gained was one-and-a-half leg lengths (the opponent's leg length), which prevented the attacker from hitting them with a step-through kick. It was pointed out that the first step should be somewhat shallow to prevent tripping yourself and that the entire maneuver was "to keep you from thinking you finished the job".

About this time some kids stuck their heads in the door of the ballroom we were having the seminar in. He asked them if they wanted to watch and maybe volunteer their bodies. They left.

As he taught *Parting Wings* he commented, "One can't pronounce a word well without knowing the definition." He went on to show how to compound the movements of the technique with insert strikes and checks. We get so wrapped up in the base movement we can't see the further potential in the moves. His analogy here was to learning how to drive a stick-shift vehicle. "You're concentrating so hard, you can't even have a conversation. Brake, gas, clutch, steering. After a while, you have the radio on, got an arm around the girlfriend – no problem. It has become second nature. That's how I want you with the movements."

As he spoke about knowing the movements well and how it took practice and thought he went into a story about the famous singer, Tom Jones. Elvis and Ed Parker went to Jones' Vegas show because Elvis wanted to be entertained. About three-quarters of the way through the show Jones made the mistake of telling the crowd that Elvis was in the audience. Parker and Elvis had to leave, and they went to Tom Jones' dressing room until the show was over. When Tom came in they had sat and talked for a while, Tom said to Elvis that he had heard that Elvis was taking karate. Elvis said he had and started to get up to demonstrate. Parker stopped him, saying that Elvis had come out to relax, so he would demonstrate. As he did techniques on some of the guys, Tom Jones lived up to his name – "Doubting Thomas". It was "What-if, but," etc. "We have a saying in my school" Parker told him. "To hear is to doubt, to see is to be deceived, but to feel is to believe" and he punched the star in the solar plexus, knocking the wind out of him. "I believe", Jones gasped.

He finished the seminar with several stories between the last two techniques to highlight his thoughts on power transfer, communication, logic, and ethics.

Parker disputed the commonly held idea that using Newton's Law of every action having an equal and opposite reaction was the best way to generate power. He believed that cocking your hand to your opposite hip while punching often left you exposed and did not provide the best positioning of available weapons. He likened the punch thrown with a high check and shuffle to an airplane being shot off an aircraft carrier. "Do they shoot the airplane off the deck and then start the engine? No! The catapult and the engine of the airplane are harmonized for maximum effort. So can you not shuffle, using your legs like the catapult to generate power? Yes! And can you have your other hand in position to shoot instead of at your hip? Like a cue ball in pool? Yes. There may not be any cue balls to hit but there are two eyeballs", he joked.

A cornerstone of the Parker system was his work in establishing a dictionary of terminology, which would later become glossaries and eventually, the *Encyclopedia of Kenpo*. He told me we should be able to talk on the phone about a technique and understand each other through the use of his precise terminology. With very few exceptions I have found this to be true. Communication is paramount. Huk Planas told me he was the guinea pig when Parker and Kelly wrote the manuals. They would read it to him to see if he moved as they wanted. Mr. Parker told a documented story about a man who bought an Indian elephant for his circus and after a week the elephant started to become difficult to manage. It became such that he decided to execute the animal and set a date to do so, and sold tickets to the event. That evening, as the crowd filled the arena, a small man approached the owner and asked if he could go in the cage with the elephant. The owner was about to refuse but then thought about what a show it would be for the spectators if the elephant killed the man, so he allowed it. The man entered the cage, spoke a language the owner had never heard, and the elephant became docile. The language was Hindustani. The elephant was Indian. The small man was Rudyard Kipling, an author famous for his writings about India. He reputedly said that the problem with the elephant was simply one of communication.

Logic is the keystone of the Parker system. Many of Ed Parker's stories and analogies had a message about logic and thinking for oneself. There were three stories he told about logic this day.

The first story was about applicants to become the King's coach driver. The first came in and said he could drive the coach safely within twelve inches of the edge of a cliff. The second bragged that he could do it within six inches. The third simply said that since the King was aboard he would stay as far from the edge as he safely could. Ed Parker's point was "Why take chances?"

The second story was about a man who came to his studio and announced that he had a "killer punch" and that he would let Parker hit him first, then punch Parker. "What kind of sense does that make?" said Parker. "If I had a four-inch knife and you had a twelve-inch knife, does that mean you would let me stab you before you stabbed me, and that as we both lay dying, that I could admit you made the bigger hole?"

His final story about logic told of a man who went on safari every year and each year he noticed one of the native carriers who always went for the largest bag while the rest of the servants went for the smallest. The third year he approached the man and asked him why he did that. The answer was, "The largest bag has the food in it. While it is heavy to start, as you eat, it gets lighter. By the end of the trip, I am carrying the lightest load." To Ed Parker, the knowledge you have taken on as a white belt is like that big, heavy bag of food. As you digest the knowledge, the easier it is to carry.

The "Father of American Karate" was a rebel in the martial arts community, and he stood out in the history of martial arts partly because of that. He met many a challenge; physical, verbal and most often by karate traditionalists. A Shotokan practitioner once told him Kenpo was not "pure". He told the man that Gichin Funakoshi studied two systems and combined them to make Shotokan, so how could it be pure? "Nothing is more pure than when pure knuckles meet pure flesh", Parker said. "In today's society when it's not who's right but who's left, we have to talk about ethics." He said a man came into his school and asked Parker what he would do if the rat-tail comb he had in his hand were a knife, (it turned out it was sharpened) and then he lunged full-force at Mr. Parker. "I side-stepped, shot a side kick, and broke his ribs. He was down on the ground and said to me, "You dirty fighter."

His final story about ethics was one in which a store owner's son came to him and said his teacher had assigned the class to talk about ethics with their parents. The father told his son that one day a lady, Mrs. Brown, who lived across the street from the store, came in and made a purchase. He gave her the proper change for her $20 bill but after she left he found that because of the newness of the bills, there were two $20's stuck together. "The question is, son, do I tell my partner, Jake, about it or not?" Parker asked the class, "What about Mrs. Brown? Doesn't she have anything to do with it? Such are ethics today."

These were rich seminars. They were taught at a time when he was formalizing his concepts and principles enough to be comprehensively set forth in writing. As in other situations I witnessed, he was thinking on his feet, and passed on a wealth of information both in physical technique and as a format for teaching. He said again those examples he used from writing, music, and speech allowed people to relate to the ideas presented. Bando master Dr. Myaung Gyi told me in conversation that when he spoke with the young Ed Parker who was in the process of creating the system that would become American Kenpo, he told Mr. Parker that he needed to use either an alphabetic, numeric, or geometric model. I believe Mr. Parker took this to heart because you see elements of all three in the system. Parker's use of the re-arrangement principle is one piece of evidence.

Private lessons

May 1981

Knives

In one of these lessons we talked about weapons and their usage. It was about this time that I first met Mike Pick at the Pasadena studio. Mr. Pick is known now as a tenth degree and heads his own association. When we got past the small talk about where we were from I asked him what rank he was. He told me he was a white belt. Mike's name came up because Mr. Parker said that Mike Pick was the person he spent the most time on his knife concepts with. I had the opportunity to experience this first-hand.

I was at the Parker home with Mr. Parker and Mike and the two of them were using me as the *uke* or "dummy" as they discussed the knife techniques. Now these were not the defense techniques they were doing, they were the knife fighting techniques. Mike showed Mr. Parker what he was working on in using the knife against the knife-wielding attacker as well as a weaponless man. I distinctly remember attacking with a straight knife thrust and Mike angled off with a hammering wrist cut while saying, "I believe I can completely take the hand off at this point." This was predicated on using the big, meaty Ed Parker fighting knife designed by master knife maker Gil Hibben, another Parker black belt and good friend to my first real Kenpo instructor, Mike Sanders.

With today's technology we can see old video of Ed Parker demonstrating his knife concepts on the Internet. These were the things he was developing at the time and he was excited about them. They proceeded to discuss and demonstrate all kinds of maiming and deadly techniques while using the knife sheath on me. Mr. Parker liked to use the sheath in place of the knife and the friction would leave red marks on skin where the cuts would have been. I had red marks all over. I remember them contouring the blade up my back in an obscure zone technique that would have been devastating. It was all impressive and educational. Later, Mr. Parker would mention he wanted to publish a book entitled *Speak with a Knife*[9], about his knife concepts and principles. He told me he decided not to publish it in order to keep the tactics out the hands of people who would misuse them. I have since seen the notes and outlines and

---

[9] When he thinking about a title he asked me if I had any ideas. I suggested *Infinite Incisions*. He didn't think that was funny.

there was some talk of publishing the book based on those notes. That has not happened.

In further discussing weapons, he firmly believed in proportioning weapons to the user just as he mandated the principle in our empty-hand art. My notes say "Weapons should be proportioned to the body to make them easier to handle relative to their intended correct usage." When I ordered my first Ed Parker fighting knife I was at his house while Gil Hibben was there. Gil traced the outline of my hand and later sent me his hand-made creation of a Mark III Parker knife. It was a perfect fit. Gil had created the knife as his black belt thesis and that Form Seven (the Seven at that time was a knife form) was NOT intended to be performed with the Parker knife, it was to be done with a dagger-type knife, much like Gil's later production, the *Silver Shadow* knife. "Knife blades should be as long as the base of the palm to finger tips" expressed one of Ed Parker's thoughts on the size of a knife.

Clubs

A story Mr. Parker would tell about proportioning weapons involved the former governor of California, Ronald Reagan, later President of the United States. Parker was on a push to get his methods taught in the police academies in the state. His argument was that each police recruit was given the same size baton even though each and every one of them had a different body size. "They are not given the same size shoes!" he would say, and therefore recommended each getting a different length of baton. That would give them the ability to manipulate the weapon efficiently for their size. He worked his way up to see the governor to make his pitch.

His ideas on using a stick or baton utilized an "upper-case, lower case" concept in which the major striking end was the upper case and the handle end, the lower. This enabled one to hook a punch with the "lower case" as you simultaneously struck with the "upper case". His idea on the club proportion was, "Clubs measure from the finger tips to the elbow so, when palmed, it protects the elbow by extending past it". When he got in to see Reagan one of the techniques he demonstrated used this. Reagan was interested enough to ask to see what he meant and got up from behind his desk. Mr. Parker had the club end palmed in his right hand so that the club was vertically parallel to and obscured by his right arm. As he described his thoughts and when the Governor was close he feinted to the groin with his right hand, which caused Reagan to bend forward to pull his hips away to avoid being hit. As he did Mr.

Parker flicked the free "upper case" end to the face, controlling the shot enough to keep from hitting Reagan and getting the bodyguards quite excited. Mr. Reagan waved them off. You could see when he told this story that he got a lot of pleasure from the reaction.

It was much later that a stick form would be taught in Kenpo schools and incorporated into the system. It is a double stick form and today goes by the name of Form Seven. However, some instructors know and teach the individual techniques Mr. Parker taught many years ago that use the principles I have mentioned here.

The staff

The staff is a popular weapon for many reasons; one being is that it seems to evoke mental images of ancient warriors, which makes it a great demonstration or tournament weapon. It is considered to be royalty among the weapons in Chinese arts.

There is a double-end staff and a single-end staff. At first the terms make no sense. After all, doesn't a staff have to have two ends? The double-end staff refers to methodology of use that largely uses both ends to strike with while the single-end predominantly uses one.

The Kenpo staff is double-ended and he said it "Measures from the ground to the eyebrows to give ground clearance". The single-end staff measures from the ground to the height of the extended arm. We use a straight staff and not a taper end staff. It is easy to buy either type today, and possibly even close to the right length, as opposed to years ago. Remember that yesterday's practitioners likely had to cut a branch from a tree and fashion it to meet their personal needs. Today, we pick up the phone and say; "I'd like to order a big stick, please".

The Staff Set done in so many Kenpo schools today is based on a longer version of a Chinese staff set done with a much longer staff. I've seen video of the long version. Like many other repetitious Chinese forms, someone took it upon himself or herself to shorten and distill the essence of the form. I've seen this in Tai chi, where shortened versions are rampant. And that is probably an influence to why we have short and long versions of Kenpo forms as well. Mr. Chuck Sullivan is credited with shortening that long version to what we do today. I'd heard the Staff Set was created in Chuck Sullivan's back yard. I spoke with Mr. Sullivan about it and he said it was true. He told me he was apprehensive about showing it to Mr. Parker and waited some time before he did, being unsure of what Mr. Parker would say. Ed Parker's reaction when he saw it? "Let's go with that."

By the way, the name, *bo,* is used in Karate to indicate a staff. To say "Bo staff" is to say "staff staff".

Sophisticated basics

I asked a kids class one day what they thought a sophisticated basic was and one answer was, "A basic that went to school". As schooling adds to a human being's essence I can see the parallel. Ed Parker had an interesting idea when he discussed basics in their embryonic and sophisticated states. Simply put, the embryonic is one move, one effect. The sophisticated is one move, two or more effects.

In having our discussions, according to my notes on these days, they were more on the fine points in basics rather than elaboration on terminology.

Over the years I have been asked about the placement of the rear foot in the execution of a drag-step shuffle. Like anything else there are two arguments. One school of thought is that if you bring your feet together you may get swept or that your balance is more of a one-point type. Therefore you should bring your feet to a point that prevents that. The other school says bring them together. It covers the most distance for this maneuver, balance can be maintained if the center of gravity is held as it should be, and it serves as the reference move for the execution of the basic. I have always taught it with the feet coming together to illustrate the basic maneuver, which is what I call the reference move. What did Ed Parker have to say about it?

"The foot placement of the drag-step shuffle is (preferably) rear arch to front heel in order to protect the groin. It may be modified to the rear heel/front arch if directional change is desired. This also makes use of the body contours."

I guess my memory served me correctly over the years. I would teach kids with a "relay race" analogy. Your feet "tag and go". Bill "Superfoot" Wallace did his famous shuffle side kick by bringing his feet together. He was a Judo man and wrestler before he did karate and he knew that you could be swept with your feet together. But there are factors not present in "free" fighting versus "hands-on" as in Judo. Bill would also float his center of gravity up as he kicked, operating on the principle that you lightened up the leg as you rose and could skip the kick in. It worked for him, and many of his students. The key here is to know that the tailoring principle is always available and you do what you need to do. But the basic gives us the reference movement from which to make those tailoring modifications.

Speaking of kicking, we talked about hip rotation while kicking.

"Hip rotation to a point parallel to the leg on a front thrust kick is essential to achieve penetration. The hip should not create a right angle to the leg."

We do front snap kicks and front thrust kicks. There are hybrid kicks, too, such as the snapping thrust. The snap doesn't need the hip rotation to the same degree as the thrust. The thrust must also have support leg rotation to prevent injury to the knee.

More on upward blocks

I wrote about his ideas on the upward block as an example of three ways to look at motion, those being the defensive, offensive defense and aggressive offense. Here he states,

"Upward blocks may be done two ways. Up the center to the chin, followed by the torque upward which blocks – almost stopping the action. Or up the center to the eyebrows, then torquing, which creates more of a ricochet effect that the first method does not have."

There is a significant difference in at least two ways to do an upward block. Most hard-style systems hold the arm at a ninety-degree angle, creating a horizontal barrier just above the head. Many systems, Kenpo included, use the diagonal application. The 90-degree version uses different muscle groups in its application and you have to be fairly strong to insure the rebound caused by the contact does not cause the arm to collapse on your own head. The diagonal version does create a deflection angle the 90-degree version does not, but doesn't work as well when used with footwork that keeps you on line with the attack, as does the other method. That's why you don't see Parker people use this block moving straight forward or back, it's always used while moving off the line. Ed Parker's descriptions of the two we use illustrate timing changes and their effect. He talked about timing changes when using a straight punch and how they merely changed the timing, not the basic principle of torque. An upward block is merely a punch on the vertical plane.

Professor Chow and the upward block

I was with him one day, driving from Pasadena to Garden Grove, (in the Cadillac Elvis gave him, by the way), and he told me a story about going to a noodle shop in

Honolulu with Professor Chow. Shortly after entering, a man approached the Professor and verbally assaulted him, saying Chow owed him money and asking when was he going to get it. The altercation degenerated to physical action when the man grabbed the Professor by the lapel with his left hand. A live demonstration of *Lone Kimono* ensued.

"The arm broke, the bones came out..." Mr. Parker related to me. This was inspirational to the young fighter. He went home and started nailing 1x2 boards to an anchoring surface and practiced breaking them with his forearms in the fashion directed in the technique.

There are two footnotes to this story. One is that the technique was not known then as *Lone Kimono.* The other is that this sort of thing (the bones coming through the skin) can and does happen with a compound fracture and that the "speed demons" in our system may not give themselves enough time to detect that and possibly injure themselves up on the broken bones. Think about each strike being the only strike. Assess its effectiveness and proceed only if necessary.

The eight directions

"The eight directions of attack and defense as indicated on the patch (both the IKKA crest and within the Universal Pattern) *are within the Zone of Directional Movement. Any target to be struck should be at the intersection of these directions."*

Mr. Parker elaborated much on zone theory in his *Infinite Insights* series. He had some interesting preliminary work that he published in *Secrets of Chinese Karate* (the S.O.C.K. book) in 1963. However, I think this one statement above really is one of the most important things anyone could know about movement. If your punch hits his chin, that's the center of the eight angles. Now picture those angles as vertical, horizontal or diagonal. If you were to move vertically from that point of contact you could strike with an elbow to the chest. If you went horizontally the target could be the jaw hinge with an inward elbow. On the diagonal plane your arm could roll into either a diagonal downward inward elbow or a spiraling outward upward elbow to the head.

The point here is that you should examine what possibilities lay within the movement at each point of contact. Each place you touch generates a new eight-angle pattern and more than one may be in use at a given time.

And when you move off one of those lines another pattern arises. He spoke of this when talking about footwork patterns in the forms. You can follow one line and when you move off to another the second pattern can be used. A pattern sprouts off a line of a previous pattern. Keep in mind that you often hit with two weapons at once and each of those becomes a central point from which to continue.

Neutral Zones

These zones are imaginary areas that you move to or that you can attack.

"The neutral zones of defense are those corners of a square surrounding a circle to which a practitioner will move (cover-out) in order to attack or defend when the opponent is in an awkward position."

The general rule here is that you move to the nearest relative 45-degree angle when you cover out, as long as that movement keeps you covered and the attacker's zones cancelled. Once you are positioned and they can't hit you, you're in the Neutral Zone of Defense.

That's the defense side of the story. The attack side is this.

"The neutral zone of attack is the zone of an opponent's body that moves the least when the opponent launches his attack. Thus, that zone will be the most vulnerable."

This doesn't say the target doesn't move. It says moves the least. If someone throws a shuffle back-knuckle at you his arms and legs move but his ribs don't move too much. So the side kick counter fits right in.

In 2023 my student, Steven White, was talking with Randy Reid. Randy was a top-rated fighter I had fought in a tournament in the late 1970s. When Reid discovered I was Steve's teacher he told Steven he remembered me because I was one of only two to beat him in competition, the other being top-ranked Dan "Superdan" Anderson of Oregon. He remembered me because of the punch I hit him with. I remember the punch because it was an example of striking that Neutral Zone. I saw everything coming at me and his chest moved the least, so I punched it. Years later, when Ed Parker told of this concept I immediately got it, having had practical experience with it. In my years with Mr. Parker I had numerous experiences that related to his principles, which convinced me his was solid thinking.

Body Momentum

Later in his books and seminars he would tie in the three zones of width, depth, and height to the power principles of torque, back-up mass, and marriage of gravity. At this time it was pretty simple and he had this to say;

"Body momentum utilizes motion in any direction to enhance the power of the strike. Back-up mass refers to the weight of the body, or portion of it, in striking."

Kenpo people love to argue about terminology and definitions. I think it's pretty simple. When you rotate you change width. That's torque. When you move forward or back you change depth. That's back-up mass. When you drop it's a height change. That's marriage of gravity. If you go up it's back-up mass because it fits the definition. What I think is important in what he said here is that he points out that it doesn't have to be the whole body. Think about a finger whip to the groin. You don't <u>have</u> to move your whole body. Often just the whip action is enough to be effective. That's what I call isolated back-up mass and it fits his definition. I call it total back-up mass when the whole body moves. Then there's directional harmony. You can't have total back-up mass if you're using opposite force. You could shuffle forward with a punch as you grab and pull the arm down. But the grab and pull is going in another direction so you don't have all your mass moving the same direction. Does it make a difference? Maybe. Ask the guy you hit.

Private lesson

February 23, 1982

My notes are sparse for this date and we apparently talked about a wide variety of things. The major/minor concept was first.

"Targets may be broken down into major and minor categories."

He liked the major/minor concept and taught it frequently when talking about block applications and striking power. With blocks he used the minor inward/major outward combination to demonstrate the idea. With strikes he called the minor the set-up move and the major was the devastating impact move. I think Huk Planas said it best when he said minor/major was to hit "hard and harder".

The trend of the lesson was toward basic fundamentals. By this time I had been working quite a bit with Frank Trejo. Mr. Parker had me learn much of the intermediate material from Frank, the purpose being three-fold. It would save him the time of having to teach me, he could crosscheck what Frank was teaching, and it would be beneficial for Frank and myself. It worked as planned and Frank and I got into some interesting discussions and hands-on work, both wanting to prove a point. At times we were lucky enough to have Mr. Parker drop in the studio while we were engaged in this often "non-verbal communication" and he would settle the "argument". There was a good reason why people wouldn't ask Mr. Parker if something actually worked. He'd show you that it did. Frank and I experienced the "laying on of hands" on many occasions. Old-timers can tell you about how we cringed when someone questioned or even challenged a technique. Most times you'd suddenly see lots of space around the guy who asked.

Frank taught me most of the Orange belt technique extensions. We were doing the *Shielding Hammer* extension when we realized that the second-to-last shot obscured the final back kick for two reasons. The first is that your hand is in the way of his line-of-sight due to the position you knocked him into. The second is that when you lean your body for the kick you also tend to drop your lower body out of his line-of-sight, too. It intrigued me so I asked about it.

"Back kicks drop the body from vertical to horizontal to improve the torque and make them less visible to the opponent."

I made a contribution to the terminology of the system when he adopted a term I used, which was "Residual torque". He agreed that the timing of the torque was different with a shovel or stiff-leg back kick. I said it felt as if the torque was delayed or leftover from the origination of the kick. It's still plain, old torque but with a name for the timing change.

We got into foot maneuvers in general and crossovers in particular.

"Front crossovers aid hand use and directional change. They also may be used as launching for the other leg. Use the contour of the body as a "homing device" to improve the accuracy of your action; the Guideline Principle."

There is a distinction between a crossover and a crossover/step-out. The crossover is technically when you cross one leg over the other. The crossover/step-out is what most people call a crossover. He'd say "Crossout to the cover" or "cover out" and mean the crossover/step-out to distance yourself mostly at the end of a technique. There are several terms in the system with multiple definitions and this is one.

I found in my travels teaching around the world that most don't realize there are four characteristics of the crossout.

First, as most know, it's to move away from the opponent so as to be in a position to keep them canceled.

Second, most know it is to scan the area, either 180 or 360 degrees, depending on the footwork (single or double cover.)

Third is to keep your weapons cocked.

And fourth is to cover your centerline.

In general you use a front crossover when you want to use both hands, and a rear crossover when you want to use primarily the front hand. The crossover was used extensively in fighting on stairs, particularly with a weapon. In the Parker system the front crossover lends itself nicely to guide-lining a follow-up knee strike with the rear leg.

Chicago seminars

April 1982

Frank Trejo and John Conway Jr., the "Irish Flash", came out from Los Angeles for the weekend. Frank and I had become good friends and John was an up and coming L.A. area competitor whose father, the late John Conway Sr., was one of the best known names in Kenpo in Ireland. The photo below is of actor Woody Strode, and Conway, Sr. and myself.

Woody Strode played in Spartacus with Kirk Douglas.

Two seminars and a tournament were scheduled for the weekend. I had asked Mr. Parker to do two seminars, one on basics and another on nunchaku. I have to say I was pretty impressed with what I saw in those two hours. He did one movement that caused both Frank and I to whip our heads around toward each other with a "Did you see that!?" coming from both of us simultaneously.

We had a pretty good crowd for this seminar, with about 30 people from several different systems attending. Gil Hibben was there, as was Herb Steet. Herb was a California black belt who relocated to Ohio, which brought him to our seminars in the Midwest. Herb later lost a leg in a motorcycle accident after he went back to California but it didn't stop him from practicing Kenpo. I saw him at a camp in Las Vegas where he was working alongside everyone else.

I opened the seminar with a presentation. One of my students, Pat Sullivan, and his wife had made a stained glass Universal Pattern and asked me to give it to him. He gracefully accepted it, used it as a visual aid for the seminar, and later had it hanging in the hallway to his office in his home. See the photo.

That day he had his right wrist wrapped but it didn't seem to slow him down. Over the years I'd see a wrist or ankle wrapped and found that he had gout, a condition that painfully affects the joints.

To start, Mr. Parker asked if there was anyone who was pretty good with the nunchakus that would care to demonstrate. Nobody offered to, so Tom McLennan was drafted. Tom was good with them and wasn't shy about getting up in front of a crowd. He worked them for a minute or so and got a round of applause. Mr. Parker took the opportunity to say that he'd seen many people who were very good with the nunchaku but were "baton twirlers". His observation was that once they met any resistance they were lost. That said, he told the group that they needed to practice hitting a heavy bag with the nunchaku to learn to overcome rebounding caused by the resistance inherent in striking. By following through with your hand making an almost linear path from a circular strike you will get penetration and not have to be overly concerned with getting hit yourself with the rebound. When he initially asked the question about why one would use a heavy bag to work on, one of the participants answered, "To make more noise". This amused the master, who said, "This guy wants louder sound" as he shrugged his shoulders. That man later came to me looking for a promotion to black belt. When I told him he wasn't ready he nodded his head, picked up his bag, and left, never to be seen in my studio again. He went off and promoted himself to black. I saw him years later wearing a fifth degree. Go figure.

As he continued on the subject of rebound he asked the class why so many people did a rebound off the inner thigh, asking, "Does it make you feel good?" The thigh rebound was actually a groin strike underneath to a man behind and he showed it by having Frank Trejo grab him. He explained that the rebounds and rolls off the body were to increase energy for re-direction to another target or even another attacker. That's when he did the rebounding off a kick that Trejo and I were impressed with. He talked about the eight basic angles in the Universal Pattern and told us to consider that there were actually 10, if you thought about the ones that came straight out or back. "But I guess you guys already knew this", he said.

Once again he raised the subject of knowing terminology and definitions. He said there was no point to learning a *kata* or a language if you don't know the definitions. A story he frequently told about his younger days in Hawaii involved teaching missionaries some Hawaiian phrases to tell the girls they were beautiful. When they actually used the phrases they got their faces slapped because the prank had been to teach them to say something to the effect that the girl was useless and ugly. The lesson here, as he explained it, was to make sure you knew the definition for the terminology, not just the terminology. This was a point he revisited frequently in his teachings.

When showing the value of forward and reverse grips with the nunchaku he asked to use some Parker knives to illustrate. (It was always interesting to see how many knives would come out at times like this.) He showed how the versatility of the forward or blade-out grip was superior to the blade-back grip and stated that it was what he preferred in using the knife. This compared to the use of the nunchaku and he favored the natural grip. He called the nunchaku a circular weapon since it has a pivot point in it at the links (strings, chains). As he got into how to change grips and hands, you could hear nunchakus dropping left and right. When he asked them to insert a kick with the swings he got so many confused looks it was rather funny. On the other hand, he often got big smiles from people in his seminars when he taught some principle or nuance, showing that they understood this new information he was sharing. He said that shooting the kick was like shooting at someone's feet with a six-shooter. "When you're dancing you're not thinking about shooting back," he said.

A point he made from time to time, and arose here, was about how someone's attitude could be affected by how you held a weapon. If a cop came into the room slapping his baton against his palm, everyone would mentally go into a defensive posture. If you held the nunchaku in your hands in front of your body, he maintained you'd get the same result. For this reason he felt you should hide the nunchaku behind your back, leg, or arm and proceeded to show a few ways to work from those positions. "Attitude breeds attitude" was how he simply put it.

He asked me to get in front of the group and teach a few self-defense techniques using the nunchaku, which was a surprise to me. It was a good thing I'd read his book. He didn't do this sort of thing too often but if you were with Ed Parker as a teacher of his art you'd better be ready to think on your feet.

In a funny moment, he mentioned that he wished he had a heavy bag to use and Tom McLennan actually had one in the back seat of his car. He brought it in and Mr. Parker had the class line up and work on striking the bag to control rebound. I didn't want to ask why Tommy had a heavy bag in his car but fate works in strange ways.

The guys were hitting the bag with the nunchakus and he was saying "Good! Great! Terrific!" as they filed through. He'd stop to correct some and make a point or two as well. He emphasized the value of common sense in what we do several times in the seminar. He wanted them to know that if they could use a principle to increase their power even by three or four percent, they were ahead. He also reinforced the different types of power that could be used, demonstrating gravitational marriage and torque with the added contributions of fulcruming and directional harmony.

As he concluded he answered some questions. Naturally people were curious as to what he thought about disarming a man with nunchakus. One man called them "numchuks" and he immediately corrected him by saying, "They're not called numchuks. Maybe the guy becomes numb when you hit him...." He proceeded to show how to use a "soft fulcrum" to go with a strike and wrap them away for a disarm. He also told them the best word in the English language was often EXIT and that would probably be the best thing to do. His final words were about how many people are really good baton-twirlers with the nunchaku but really couldn't use them in application. He related a story about a Chinese man who approached him at the Internationals and wanted to know why the Grand Champion in form only got $100 and the Grand Champion in freestyle would get $350. He replied that the freestyle champ faced hazards; he might get a rib cracked, teeth knocked out, or his nose broken. Unless the forms man tripped and hurt himself there was little or no hazard. The man couldn't accept that so he said, "Have you ever seen a world champion shadow boxer?" The man bowed and thanked him.

In the basics seminar he drilled a lot on foot maneuvers and spoke of consistency of principles. He insisted that television was the reason we were conditioned to wind up our punches. We'd watch TV and see people constantly wind up to punch and we copied it.[10] He wanted us to strike from point of origin and that was what he worked the group on, combining their strikes with foot maneuvers. Once again he told us that techniques could be done differently from person to person and they'd be correct as long as the principles were kept to, therefore the consistency of principle comment. He used an example of handwriting, describing how we copy a penmanship teacher's example, but never get it to look exactly the same. It would be legible and distinguishable but not exactly like hers. That was how he described the difference between system and style. <u>What</u> we copied was the system, <u>how</u> we copied was the style. Another interesting example of consistency was when he said, "If we jump off a cliff we die unless we use a hang-glider. It's use of another over-riding principle that allows us to do it."

---

[10] He called it the John Wayne Syndrome. His argument was that we saw it time and again and thought that was the way we were supposed to punch. Television and movies actors use such methods due to camera angles and it helps the audience member perceive that the punch is about to be thrown.

In a further analogy to system and style he told us that in as a carpenter California if he wanted to drive a nail in with a hammer he'd hit straight up and down. "Then I find myself in Chicago and they tell me I have the right idea but it needs to be done with a circle going from inside to outside. I go down to Florida and they tell me I'm doing it wrong and have to make the circle from outside to inside. Finally I go home to Hawaii and they say "Hey Bruddah, whatcha doin'? You gotta hold the hammer upside down and pound the nail in"." He stated that the system, that being the nail and hammer were constant; it was the method of execution of using the hammer that made style.

As he discussed stances he said that people "look at stances as being different monsters. But they're all tied in and related". He discussed the proper proportions for each and their similarities and differences. He added the maneuvers to them, along with some strikes and encouraged them as they got the message. When he observed many of them breaking at the waist or actually straightening their front leg when going to a forward bow he said, "I'm going to have to put a tail-light on your butt" and told them to keep themselves aligned correctly for maximum back-up mass. He drilled them some more and when he saw improvement commented, "Not bad. You can open your eyes now." Some of these guys were trying so hard they couldn't do it right because they were in the presence of the master and he recognized that. Watching him work, how he related to the younger students and involved them, what effect his questions and explanations had, and how the group was engaged by his presentation, one could certainly understand the effect Ed Parker had on karate practitioners everywhere.

He mentioned that a well-known martial artist, who would remain nameless, said that the crossover foot maneuver was useless. "Maybe in a ring, but not in the street" was his answer.

Once again ethics were raised. He liked to say that as in boxing, where ethical boxers kept all blows above the belt, Kenpo is ethical, too. "We keep all blows above the soles of the feet. And we never kick a female in the testicles." Such were Ed Parker's ethics for defense in the street.

Conway Jr, Trejo, Wedlake, Parker, Hibben and others

As in many other seminars both here in Chicago and elsewhere around the world, he used some of his favorite techniques to re-emphasize how to think. He once again did *Five Swords* to show how it didn't really matter which arm the opponent threw, the pattern could pick it up and handle it. He said, "Look upon an arm as an arm, not as a right or a left." *Parting Wings* was once again used to show how to fill movement with inserts. He did seminars so often and in so many places he tended to get repetitious sometimes. As I watched the tapes so many years later I saw that he did these techniques frequently in Chicago and it led to diminishing attendance toward the end of the 80s. He told the class that two things were important to know and those were that they needed to think about intentional and unintentional moves on the part of the attacker. He spent time emphasizing check positions in the two techniques and got them to work faster and harder. At first they were not moving as fast as he'd like so he said, "Grandma moved faster than that on the day she died." His humor helped loosen up a class and relax them. A relaxed student usually learns better. He had a gift that allowed him to work with a group and make them feel like he was just one of the guys and was letting them in on something. The jokes, pithy comments, war stories, and analogies made an Ed Parker seminar memorable.

At a tournament I held in Chicago

Frank had just knocked down Harold "Scorpion" Burrage at that same tournament.

Photo by Brad Crooks.

Signed by Ed Parker, Mills Crenshaw, Steve Armstrong, Steve Fisher, the #1 fighter in U.S. at the time and student of Mike Stone

Tom Kelly – Ed Parker's right-hand man

Promoted by Trejo and Planas to 7th degree

Private lesson

December 1982

I have with my notes lists of questions I asked him. Some are just the list with no answer, and others I wrote down the answer. As I look at them over 25 years later, the ones with no answers are common knowledge, or maybe just stupid questions. These following notes cover miscellaneous questions and their answers.

Ed Parker chose his words carefully and his definitions were the result. There are some examples of the wrong word being used and those are largely due to the common understanding, or misunderstanding really, of some words in the English language. One thing about his definitions is that he was the first to create a workable set of terms, so much so that other systems and practitioners adopted them. The martial arts historian the late John Corcoran included them in his martial arts glossary that he published monthly in one of the magazines he used to edit with an (EP) next to them to credit him.

I asked Mr. Parker about the terms orbital <u>change</u> and orbital <u>adjustment</u>.

"Orbital adjustments differ from orbital changes in that a <u>change</u> involves the eight basic angles and an <u>adjustment</u> involves the degrees between the angles."

He would often use the word "switch" instead of change. What he was telling me here is that if the change was less than 45-degrees it was an adjustment.

It bears repeating that the eight angles are the simplest way to get a feel for direction. There are 360 degrees in a circle. You'd go nuts trying to work with terms that were so precise in angle that you'd be trying to describe something like, "Move your foot to 004° and strike across on the 274°-094° line". The clock principle works just fine for what we do. We do want to be precise but this would take it out of the realm of practicality for most people and applications.

I've been told some think the clock principle is outdated, as many children today are used to digital clocks and can't read a clock with hands. I have surveyed instructors and the predominant answer is that the majority can and they teach the rest how. Simple. However, there are words we've used that are becoming outdated and need explanation today, such as telegraphing and phone booth.

I asked him, "What hits harder? A punch or a heel-palm strike?" He said the heel-palm hits harder because there are less joints and bones involved to absorb force. When you look at his techniques you see a predominance of open hand strikes. I haven't done a statistical analysis but I think it would prove out mathematically and it reflects this belief.

A related question was "Does an elbow hit harder than a punch?" The elbow will strike harder than a punch because it follows the same axis of rotation as the rest of the body (directional harmony). A punch rotates on an axis 90-degrees from the body.

"What are brother-sister-cousin moves?" They all stem from the same base move. They are changes in the angle of delivery from a particular starting position. Example – left inward block with the rear hand cocked. The rear hand can punch straight, angle up to the head, down to the groin, or become an elbow instead of a punch.

Now here were some interesting subjects. We got to talk about sensitivity, circular motion, and *chi*, the life force.

"Our self-defense techniques act as a form of chi-sao (sticky hands). *When contact is made, the position of parries, blocks, strikes, checks, etc will allow us to have sensitivity to the moves of the opponent. This is part of the reasoning behind the overkill principle. When the*

techniques teach extensions they introduce or reinforce a repertoire of moves that can be utilized spontaneously as needed to take advantage of all the body positions. The techniques should flow together. The techniques use circular motion to retain chi."

I thought that was all very interesting, especially the comment about *chi*. I had asked it because I had been exposed to a trick in which you "steal" someone's *chi* by sliding your hand along their arm repeatedly as if stroking it. As I later found, that was in the reverse direction of their *chi* flow. The body has what is called a microcosmic orbit and the arms and legs each have their own particular path of energy flow. Without getting into a whole discussion of the yin and yang sides of the body and limbs and if you have some working knowledge of the internal arts, you'll see that the Kenpo techniques generally follow the opponent's outflow directions and your inflow directions. That leads me to believe what he said is true, that the movements help us retain our *chi*.

Finally, we got to talk about the Analysis of Technique, which later became the Three Phases - ideal, what –if? and formulation. What he called Phase One referred to fixed situations, the ideal technique. I remember him saying that he constructed the techniques with "One, two, or maybe even <u>three</u> principles in mind!" In later years I would see in one of the *Infinite Insights* books, a picture of one move with about 14 arrows pointing out various principles and concepts. That's not what he was doing when I first worked with him. He was more focused on the most important factors and some elements became more complex as the years went by. That's not bad; it just clouds the picture for some. First year high school science students don't speak technical English like an engineer might and first year Kenpo students don't speak technical Kenpo like an instructor.

The Second Phase became the "What-if?" phase. In my notes he calls it "prediction of consequence". He liked to talk about how people were so anxious to jump right from the first phase to the second with a "What if I do this?" type question without having a grasp of the basic principles in the technique. The whole "What-if?" is interesting because it should also be looked at from all three perspectives. He emphasized the three points of view - that of the defender, the attacker(s), and the bystander. He believed that when you considered these, your understanding would increase many times. We should look at the situation with an eye to changing the weapon, timing, target, force, etc. and be able to predict what the reaction would likely be to these alterations. This ties in to what you can do to a technique (prefix, suffix, add, alter, insert, rearrange, regulate, delete).

Phase Three he called actual application or combat training and later was known as Formulation. He said it was the "formal equation". It is on-the-spot application of what you know. You have to take what you have and mix it to create something immediately workable, hence the term "formulate", which has as part of its dictionary definition, "to devise".

Chicago Seminars

May 1983

In the first edition of this book I had overlooked these two seminars, had a timeline gap and have added a recap here.

In the beginner seminar video it is apparent by his interactions he loves children and arranges the lines so the kids and smaller adults could be up front. He started with talking about the importance of terminology and a question got him on the subject of style versus system. Earlier in this book I wrote of our discussion about it but here he explained it using his analogy to famous painters. He asked the group what Picasso, Van Gogh and Rembrandt had in common. He pointed out that all three used a canvas, brush and paint. That was the system. The fact that all their work looked quite different indicated various styles in application of the system.

He went on to us our chalkboard and describe his motion chart. He'd elaborate of use of height, width and depth and proportioning stances to your body- tailoring. Watching the video, you can see he was confusing people. He teased them, telling them there would be a quiz. One would tell me later, "He was pretty abstract". He walked among the group, spoke of the parallels in martial arts and life lessons and how everyday motion could be used in defense.

"You're starting to think!" he exclaimed when he asked a question and got the right answer. When one said "I think so", his response was "Do you think or do you know?" That triggered a story.

He told of a man, high on drugs, who came into the studio and challenged him. "I think I can beat you" he said. Mr. Parker asked, "Do you think or do you know?" The man said he knew, was happy and left. However, he returned another time, started with the same question, and a fist-fight ensued with the manager and a student. I heard this story before, Trejo was the student and Steve Herring was the manager. It got wild, the Kenpo people busted him up pretty well and threw him down the front stairs. Mr. Parker told the group the man then took of his clothes and walked down the street. Trejo told me he did push-ups at the bottom of the stairs, stood up and saluted, and walked off. He did say the man disrobed inside the studio, though. I was not sure I believed the story even after hearing it from Frank and Mr. Parker. But when I was teaching in Dallas many years later I met a couple who actually witnessed it.

He followed by saying we had a drug problem in the country. We still do today. He remarked that people on drugs are very difficult to deal with and that's absolutely true.

Examining motion, discussing opposites and reverses, referring to what we call General Rules such as blocking above the elbow on the outside of a punch for example and reiterating major and minor moves followed. He wanted to demonstrate meeting motion to beat motion and asked, "Who has fast hands?". "You do!" was an answer from the crowd.

His main point for this seminar was that most "do not have a full knowledge of motion". Answers are found when you change your perspective.

In the advanced seminar he spent time discussing and demonstrating his concepts of inserts and many other principles. Most of them were done using *The Back Breaker* to illustrate. He was emphatic on many points and today, when I watch online videos of practitioners doing the technique, what I see is most I've seen did not get the message.

Chicago Seminars

November 1983

We spent a day working on forms, Short and Long One, Short Two, the Finger Set, Short Three and Long Three. Of course, the Finger Set is not a form but a set. Ed Parker told the group in passing that there was a Short Four, and how to do it.

This group was composed of locals, a group of Ohio Tracy's people and some Shorin-Ryu practitioners. I believe this was the seminar I met Don MacKay from New Hampshire. Don was living in Iowa, taking Shorin-Ryu, and he and his teacher had come to attend the seminar. When Don later moved back to New Hampshire he would initiate the connection between myself and other New England practitioners who were starting to learn the Parker system, introducing me to Steve White, who was instrumental in the growth of Parker Kenpo in New England. Steve was only months behind Tony and Doreen Cogliandro in study of the Parker system and only for a short time. The couple was the other half of the New England IKKA connection with Steve.

Gil Hibben was there from Louisville, Kentucky and was introduced by Mr. Parker at the beginning of the first seminar. He mentioned with a chuckle that Gil had created the Parker knife and that he now had versions one, two, and three available. While he urged the group to look at what Gil had for sale he said there was a knife there that was "the delight of a rabbi". Throughout the seminars he would tease Gil and I, plug Gil's knives, and relate back to common experiences he and Gil had of living in Utah.

He'd spend about an hour covering Short Form One but in that time he'd re-tell stories and analogies he'd used in previous seminars and written about in his books. While he had a canned presentation, as do many traveling seminar speakers in many disciplines, he would tailor it to the group and spice it with his own humor that would keep the group laughing. When it came to asking for volunteers he'd laugh and say that the brown and black belts "no speakee Englee" and so would grab the newer guys to demonstrate on.

He started the first seminar with the importance of proportioning your stance through the use of proper height, width, and depth being reinforced, as were the elimination of "jet lag" and bobbing, and keeping the knees bent to facilitate movement. He made mention that keeping a knee locked required a one-quarter beat delay in movement and that while many may think that was not important, it is. His message today was about saving time and having poise in movement. It would take time, he said, to re-formulate habits using new principles. He told two stories to illustrate.

Back in the late 1950s and early 1960s he said he had many people stopping by his studio on their way back from Japan. One was a serviceman, 6'7" tall, who had studied karate in Japan. When asked to drop into his stance he was down in a very long and low stance. Mr. Parker asked him why and he said it was because he had been told to keep his head at the same level as everyone else in class. Raising his stance would take some practice.

Bruce Lee had told the second story to him, about a man who went to study with a new master. The master asked the man to show him what he had learned from his old master, which he did. He then showed the man a sequence and requested that he go and practice it both right-handed and left, and to meet him back on the spot in one year. A year later they met again and the master asked him to show him if he had, in fact, practiced what he had been shown. The man did so and was complimented in his progress. The master then asked him if he would show him again what he had learned from the previous master. The reply was that he had practiced so much what he had been shown that he forgot everything the first master had taught him. "Good", was the answer, "now we can start." Ed Parker was asking the class to forget some of the bad habits they had.

To drive his points home he broke Short Form One down by teaching the footwork first, then the hands. He told the class to visualize that he had a Walt Disney pen that could write in the air so they could visualize the zones of defense and the lines he wanted them to follow. He also used a Hibben knife to show proper angles of delivery for an inward block because holding the knife improperly emphasized the incorrect angles when you would see the blade turned inward instead of outward or downward.

A discussion of anchoring the elbows, using his "squeegee" description for margin for error and path of action versus line of action concepts followed. He wanted you to be sure you understood that all this was a point of reference and that height, depth, surface to be used, etc., could be altered when needed. Use of minors and majors was reiterated as he told the story again of how he discovered reverse motion by being too lazy to rewind a film clip of himself.

"Let me see your interpretation of an upward block", he requested of the group. As always, he stated he wanted the block to go up the center and shoot outward. And as he demonstrated how not to do an upward block he'd say, "Hey, mister! Let me help you bring my hand to my head" showing how too often students bring the block backward as they finish the motion. He then started to mimic banging his head against the wall as he said he was hoping they "would get it". His point was that the retracting motion down the centerline was also a momentary protective measure just as an inward block was when executing more than one vertical outward block. These corrections and instructional methods are used by many of the first generation black belts in teaching the basics.

Going into the second part of the first seminar on Long One he got a bit off track and started a discussion of Short Two as he was calling it Long Form One. The video shows me stepping to tell him that and he had me do the form for the group. Looking at it 25 years later I see the mistakes I made back then and how I was in transition between what I had learned from my previous teachers to what he wanted me to do. There was an incorrect step, lack of emphasis on some movement and an extra shift or two. It was good enough to win trophies but still wasn't right. Like he said in the first hour, it would take time to re-formulate habits.

While teaching this form he used an illustration of having me stand by a wall, putting my foot flat on the wall and pushing off with a punch to get them to think about using the floor as a brace for power. He said Long Form One was to help develop power, depth, and stability. Contouring was also described when he told the class they needed to follow the contour of their ribs to generate power in a punch. Following their own body contours helps to prevent energy from going off in divergent directions.

What was really interesting to watch was how he seemed to cover up a mistake in teaching the transition between the outward and upward block sections. Someone asked him whether it should be an outward elbow, the upward block and punch or if it was an inward, then upward and punch. He told them to use an inward, the upward and punch but qualified it by saying it should be done that way because it was "less confusing". Well, that confused people. In fact, he didn't do it like that in the video – he did the elbow, block, punch combination and said the group should go home and work on that. I think he just made a mistake and covered it. He did not cover the second section of the form, reason unknown.

We went on to Short Form Two, which he did quickly as I co-taught the class and he stepped in to reiterate some points he always mentioned in his seminars. "I do not believe in following Newton's Law", he said and went into his thoughts on shuffling to compensate for drawing back the opposite arm while punching to gain power from opposite force. I mention this again because it's quite a dramatic statement for an instructor to make.

"The fastest man in the world came into my school. He said he could block anything I threw. I asked him if he could block a left and a right. He said he could so I threw it and he blocked them. "Wow, you're pretty fast", I said." Mr. Parker made motions near his head of an expanding head, indicating the guy's ego getting to him. "I asked him if he could block a right, then a left. I threw them and he blocked them." The head gets bigger. "I asked him if he could block a left with a right and Bam! I hit him! You see, he didn't quite hear me say <u>with</u> when I said it. There is a big difference between <u>with</u> and <u>and</u>." He told this story as he showed the timing change of the block with a punch in Short Two to make his point. He made a few more points about Short Two but really didn't spend much time on it although he did re-emphasize his point about cutting through the body when doing a chop. It was at this time that

John McSweeney came in and Mr. Parker introduced him to the group. The "Father of Irish Karate" was given a round of applause and Mr. Parker told them that John was one of the guys he had "eating rusty nails". The Chicago seminars always had interesting people in attendance, as you may have gathered from your reading so far.

The Finger Set was the next subject. There was not much time spent on it, being a short set and he was finishing the first session.

The changes in height, width, and depth created by the rotation of the hands at each zone and the change of reach by a hand length was shown with the initial finger thrusts. As he progressed to the finger whips he called them flicks, along other moves such as the slices in the set. While the terms had been standardized as whips, flicks, slices, rakes, etc. well before, he liked to call them flicks.

When teaching he would remarkably change smoothly from the standard execution to mirror image methods to help the students. "Make available every weapon you can use as the opportunity presents itself. These aren't majors but they make him easier to pick at", he said as he described the whips, slices, and rakes. The ability to double-factor was shown as he struck with a chop then went to an eye-slice or hit with a heel-palm then raked the eyes with a claw.

"Why come back doing nothing when I could come back doing something?" was his comment as he demonstrated on a white belt in the front row.

From today's perspective it is interesting to watch him as he runs through the set. There are no covers or crane hooks between sides, no double underhand groin shots, and the like as are found in written descriptions of the set. Was he hiding something? Was he just glossing over movements? Had he forgotten things? There's no way to know today. All we can do is practice what we were taught, as long as it has sound reasoning behind it.

He opened the Short Three seminar with the question, "Who knows Short Three?" Not many hands went up because I used to fry my guys when they raised their hands indicating they knew the form. I would say, "How is it you know the form and I don't?" That generated many a quizzical look. I'd use it as an object lesson in how we are always learning something and don't know everything. So we tended to say we were familiar with a form rather than knowing a form, therefore the lack of raised hands. Mr. Parker picked up on that immediately and asked who knew *of* the form and many more hands went up.

As he guided them through the opening moves he asked the group if it was all right that he described techniques in his detailed manner. This is a great technique that helps people feel more at ease with the instructor, showing that he realized how nervous people could be with him around and that they would learn better when they relaxed.

Detailing as he went along, he mentioned the old stand-by phrase that "We never hit a man who wears glasses" as he showed the application of the twin finger-flick that opens *Crashing Wings* in the form. He showed how we lift the glasses with the fingers and poke the eyes with the thumbs, dropping the glasses back in place when we finish, since we are "conscientious". He also re-stated it is important to know what you're doing on every move, saying "Those who know how will be students. Those who know why will be instructors."

He did the form with the class, and when he wasn't moving, but observing, he leaned on a staff, his chin resting upon his hands stacked on the top end. At one point he complimented the class, telling them that they were moving better already, and "With authority and finesse." Sometimes it just takes a teacher a little care and the right attitude to get substantial results in a short time.

"Every move counts. If it gets 5-10% more, take it", he said as he made corrections. Effort was put into making sure the attendees understood certain principles he elaborated on, using the form techniques to drive home the points. "Who do you think of first when doing a technique? Three pronouns; me, my, I." He wanted elbows anchored, smaller circles in some moves, weight dropped with other movements, and contours to be followed. In the technique, *Fatal Cross*, the defender hooks the opponent's arms to deflect the attack. Yet, he pointed out, too many people use incorrect alignment in the hooking movement. He grabbed a "volunteer" and had him do the hooks. When he did, Mr. Parker re-orbited his arms and caught him with a double ear slap, which, understandably, quite surprised the young man. As he did so many times in so many places, he cautioned the group to be aware they not put something in motion that could re-orbit back to them. A few minutes later, after covering another move or two, he asked the student if his ears were still ringing. He got an affirmative answer and said, "Leave it alone. It will clear up by next week." Everyone, including the volunteer, laughed.

The final session on Long Form Three was very general. He worked on some detail but not much. It was interesting to watch the different ways the Tracy people did the form compared to the Parker people. The Tracy practitioners used larger circles, were missing moves, and didn't have applications or explanations for much of the movements.

The Tracy people in the group were from different parts of the Midwest, so the differences cannot be attributed to a particular instructor. But, they were there and learning the same information as the Parker guys.

He cleaned up the form and said he was happy with it by the end of the session. Along the way he gave some tips on how to remember certain movements, the wrist grab isolation in the very first technique, for example. He said, "I'll bet you remember this!" as he described the movements as circling a female breast, caressing it, and "dabbing" the nipple with a backfist. Sure enough, the guys got the motion sequence, and everyone had a laugh. The group was composed entirely of men when he did this, and I'm certain he'd not have done it with women present. In the 21st century I'm certain he also would have been accused as being politically incorrect or sexist. But the guys understood the motion and duplicated it with the applications for the wrist grab escape. You can't argue with success.

One transition was different than what I was taught but that was not uncommon in a seminar situation. Sometimes he was forgetful and sometimes he wanted to see if people challenged what he taught.

He stated that ideas of motion and movement were contained in the forms and that many of the motions were hidden moves. He used the inserts in *Parting Wings* as an example, demonstrating the slice, rip, and rake he liked to use in the technique.

Mr. Parker went on to mention the clockwise and counter-clockwise motions in the mid-way isolation, a hint to answers to many questions, as I would find later. Understanding that particular section was eye-opening for me and provided many answers later.

"Go through the motions with dignity", he said when he asked the class to run the form in its entirety. "If you don't know them, fool me. Make me think you know what you don't know." He wanted you to run the forms with confidence, just as you could see that in him when he did them.

Chicago Seminars

May 1984

It was a nice spring day in Chicago that normally would draw people outside on a weekend but we had a crowd in my studio anyway. Mr. Parker was in for his semi-annual visit to teach two seminars. The first was on multiple attackers and the second covered Form Four.

In the first session he used only one standard technique, *Falcons of Force*. The rest were combinations he used to illustrate his concepts, theories, and principles. He asked the class if they knew the difference between a concept and a theory. "A concept is an idea. A theory is an idea you're working on", he said.

He used several of the terms he was developing and mentioned his fifth volume of the *Infinite Insights into Kenpo* series as he did, saying these terms would be included in the books.

The initial combination was used to illustrate his ideas on environment, planned reaction, compounding, and amplification. He started by setting up a situation with opponents front and behind, and showing what he wanted the defender to do. As he progressed he questioned the group, took their suggestions, and built a technique as he explained what was working and why. He did this three times in the seminar, with the second one being for opponents at the sides and the third for three attackers. He showed variations as a part of the "what-if?" phase and emphasized the use of logic "to determine what you want to create in terms of reaction."

As he moved around, he showed he was still agile, fast, and powerful.[11] The faces of those in attendance were smiling as he worked his "volunteers" over. His mood was good, the jokes flowed, and stories cemented the action.

He spoke of becoming a bodyguard to punk-rock star Billy Idol and how he "had him convinced" about the system, so much so that Idol was going to have the Kenpo crest tattooed on his back. He would shortly thereafter let that connection go. Bruce Lee was also mentioned. Lee came up because of an explanation about how he related motion to three states of matter, those being solid, liquid, and gaseous. He had been interviewed for a magazine article and was upset because the interviewer was

---

[11] I asked John McSweeney if Mr. Parker had slowed down any since when he trained with him and he told me he was "just as fast".

explaining to him what Bruce Lee meant with his philosophies. Parker and Lee had spent much time together and Mr. Parker felt he had a pretty good idea what Bruce was thinking through their conversations. This led to his saying that some motion was like solid matter, other motions like liquid or gas. "Bruce preferred the liquid state. But that doesn't mean he could not work in the gaseous", he said. He told the group that a liquid seeks its level while a gas seeks its volume. Ed Parker loved to seek his volume, exploding in many directions in thought and action.

When speaking of the terminology he employed he told a story about a young man who got his face slapped for asking his girlfriend if she wished to engage in bisexual inter-digitation. "He got his face slapped for asking to hold her hand" he joked. But he followed with this lesson, "But don't slap any faces if you don't understand the terminology."

He spoke of economy of motion and said that it must be accompanied by having the desired effect otherwise it wasn't economical. If it wasn't, he said, you better have economy of *locomotion*. "Jet lag" was brought up again, as it had been in previous seminars. He thought that people who moved their face forward while moving back either "had suicidal tendencies" or "were hoping that the result of getting hit might improve their looks."

Throughout, he reinforced his ideas on using one opponent to blockade others and emphasized how one needed to be very familiar with movement and principles so that answers would flow spontaneously. He told the group that he found he did techniques that he swore he'd never do in actual situations. I'd had my own students say that they would never do some technique only to find that when the chips were down that was exactly what they did. The lesson is "never say never". He also reminded the class that his lawyer had told him to remember the phrase, "But officer, he attempted to hit me first" as he illustrated how we see an attack and can cancel it before it lands.

He closed the seminar with a story he used to illustrate the correlation of motion to language. A mother mouse was with her baby, foraging in an alley when the local alley cat approached. She had her baby get behind her, and as the cat was about to spring and devour what he thought was to be his lunch, the mother mouse barked! The startled cat turned and ran and the mother mouse said to her child, "Son, let that be a lesson in the value of a second language." He went on to say that he thought Kenpo should be like a second language to the student, a language of motion.

The second seminar was another two hours, punctuated by him doing sections of the Form Four at speed and demonstrating portions on participants. As I watched the video I saw myself making the same mistakes I correct with students today. It's a bit embarrassing but the fact that I'm much better at it today than I was in 1984 makes me feels better.

Most of the seminar was spent on working sequence, timing, and positions. He could have spent much more time on detail but with a short amount of time he hit the important points. I could go into quite a bit here but I wrote a book entitled *Kenpo Karate 401 – Form Four* that goes into depth and detail, some of which was covered in this class. In 2015 my forms books, *Kenpo Karate 101* through *Kenpo Karate 601* were consolidated into *The Kenpo Karate Compendium*, published by Blue Snake Books.

Looking back, it was interesting to see how agile his footwork was at the time. I believe this was before the gout affected his performance. In addition, he did something he did not normally do when being filmed. In many videos I have seen of seminars in some schools he positions himself so that the camera cannot see what he is doing. At this seminar he actually pulled his volunteer into position while saying "so the camera can see".

Certain parts of the form are different from what is commonly taught today. Some of the angles of delivery are different, a shuffle here or there has been added or deleted, and he does no big circle for the underhand strike in *Unwinding Pendulum*. He emphasized that contouring has two basic categories, those being contact and non-contact. He called them guidelining and tracking at the time. In the next years he would expand those with finer distinctions.

There were two standout comments he made during this seminar. The first was "You can change it all you want later but first you must understand the form." I believe this is extremely important. Too many people have changed techniques and forms without truly understanding the underlying principles and what he was intending to show. This has lead to many mutations of sequences and alteration of principles. If you understand the reasons and can demonstrate that you do, it is fair to have license with the moves. I feel that if you do and can teach the reference movements and the related information, you can alter as much as you want. I teach that way and insist that while the students do their variations they must also be able to show the standard. In this way we can keep the system intact yet still allow the freedom of expression he valued so much. I think we should add to but not take away from the system.

The second important comment he made was, "People always want more, not realizing you have more than you can cope with to start off." To drive the idea home he had us do the Star Block, also known as Blocking Set One. We did the basic way, and then backwards, then with offset timing – all things that are/were written down but many passed over in practice. It's funny how most of us grin and laugh when someone has us do something that screws us up. There was a lot of that that day. I think it's our realization that there is more to it than meets the eye that elicits that reaction. I have found it to be absolutely true that there is so much in the system he created that is obscured yet has signposts pointing the way, and he gave us the keys to find them.

He had us run the form from beginning to end and told us it was looking better than when we started. Many instructors don't compliment or encourage. He did, we appreciated it, and we improved as time went by.

Wendy's® Midwest Martial Arts Seminars

July 7-8, 1984

That's right – Wendy's®, the hamburger people. An Indiana man who was the executive vice-president of the chain and had a child in the arts sponsored the event. The child's teacher, Sensei Barry Moyer, was the coordinator. They held it in LaPorte, Indiana at the fairgrounds.

The line-up consisted of Ed Parker, Aaron Banks, Eric Lee, Billy Blanks, Ernie Reyes, Jeff Arnold and Mike Replogle, Ronald Duncan, Tadashi Yamashita, Don Wrobel, and Ted Tabura. Aaron Banks was well known for his *Oriental World of Self-Defense* that was held at Madison Square Garden and broadcasted on the ABC network show, *The Wide World of Sports.* Eric Lee was an excellent kung-fu practitioner and competitor, Billy Blanks was the up and coming nationally ranked fighter, Arnold and Replogle were the founders of the American Arnis Foundation. Ronald Duncan was a ninjutsu master, Don Wrobel a jiu-jitsu man, and Ted Tabura was called "The Sickle Man" due to his expertise with the Okinawan *kama*.

Tadashi Yamashita was one of the best weapons men in the US and used to take an apple out of a guys teeth, blindfolded, with a nunchaku. Ernie Reyes had been a Top Ten competitor and director of the dynamic West Coast Demo Team and his son Ernie Jr. was starting to be noticed. Ernie Jr. would later play in movies and be a top competitor himself. He was about eight or so then and break-dancing was the fad. Ed Parker, Ernie Jr. and Sr., myself and two others were coming out of the hotel elevator when little Ernie started "breaking" in the hallway. Mr. Parker watched him and said "Just when you think you've seen everything they come up with a new method of motion".

Mr. Parker had called me to see if I could be there, so I went and brought along Pete Tomaino and Tom McLennan. I remember enjoying the weekend, mainly because we had a lot of time to hang out with Mr. Parker. He only taught one hour-and-a-half seminar each day, leaving some dead time. He did some privates, I think, and some hobnobbing. He'd brought his ukulele and played it for us outside at a picnic bench. Tom and I helped him out with a demo or two over the weekend, one in which Tom ran into a Parker heel-palm to the nose that drew some blood. That was the price Tom had to pay for having the title of Ed Parker's adopted son. He wasn't truly adopted but the Old Man liked him and laughingly referred to that way.

The meal times were fun, having so many of those masters there at the table, and Ed Parker was the center of attention. In fact, over the weekend each one of the other instructors acknowledged Ed Parker for what he had done for them and the arts.

The sponsor had us over to his mansion-sized house one evening. In typical Ed Parker fashion, when he was invited to the house he told the host he had to bring us along. Tadashi Yamashita came with us, but none of the other teaching staff were there. We were fed and entertained with a private fireworks showing. Our host sat talking with Mr. Parker for quite some time, taking full advantage of having such a man present. We felt special being there.

The event was not as well attended as they had hoped. It was a bust, but for us it was great. Billy Blanks laughed as Tom cartwheeled for us (Billy had a big Afro hairdo and was missing his front teeth then, so I was surprised to see how he looked years later with the advent of Tae Bo), Tadashi tortured Tom, and we talked with the rest of the instructors. Once again I was grateful to be a part of Ed Parker's group.

Chicago Seminars

October 1984

Ed Parker had been coming to Chicago now twice a year for about four years. He knew many of my guys there by first name, which was a characteristic of his that made so many people the world over so comfortable with him. Had the Hawaiian royal lineage still been in power, he'd have been a prince. In my mind, that technicality didn't matter – he really was a prince and had the qualities.

He did two seminars that day. It is on the video, in the Form Five seminar, that he actually rolls up his pant leg and shows off the scars in his knee from someone's teeth. He did this because he had just demonstrated *Hopping Crane* on Jim Lowell and came very close to his face. He said, "Don't worry, I'm not going home with your teeth in my foot". That's when he showed the scars. You may think that is interesting, disgusting, or not important. But the lesson, one I have taught for years, was something he then elaborated on by saying, "Have you ever seen what happens from hitting the mouth? The infection?" and he mimed his leg expanding with his hands. "I can talk but not walk and he can walk but not talk; no teeth in his mouth" was his comment. I was told early in my youth not to punch anyone in the mouth because "He goes to the hospital and three days later you go to the hospital". It's good advice. The human mouth harbors huge amounts of bacteria and when you cut your skin hitting the teeth, the bacteria have open season, resulting in infection. Any technique you do must consider this when you get near his face. Some people are animals and will bite you. There are ways to get your hands in their mouth for purposes of tearing but it's risky and if you get bitten you should immediately get treatment.

While teaching the session on Form Five he also addresses another aspect of injury to self during a technique. His question was, "Why do nonsensical movement or positions? The purpose of this is to protect yourself, not do yourself injury". This was brought on by his observation that some people in the group did not form their hands correctly and that can lead to ineffective technique and injury. (Jeff Speakman told a story about taking a class with Tom Kelly at which Mr. Kelly asked everyone to form a heel-palm and hold it up in the air. Most of the class has their hands formed incorrectly; thumbs out, fingers splayed. "That's not a heel-palm!" he thundered, and rightly so. It's a good way to get hurt.) Now Mr. Parker went on to describe why he held his hands in such a manner when he chopped. He went into margin for error and how the chop can become an eye slice and how a heel-palm to the head can allow one to slip a thumb into the eye.

That lecture led to a demonstration of contouring. And he described how when he used a knife, once he made contact any move the opponent made allowed him to cut. "Thank you, thank you very much", he said as he contoured the blade along my body while I made attempts to escape. He liked to say, "Once you make contact you're in love" and "Every move he makes, he's your ally". The principles behind his sliding, rolling, burdening, and hugging checks, for example, are based on this. It was Ed Parker's ability to use such statements to drive his message home that made sense to almost everyone. He would get you to laugh. Public speaking coaches say that if you can get your audience to laugh they are paying attention. Mr. Parker's use of analogy was outstanding. His examples were things he could get anyone to relate to, and if they relate, then they can understand. If they understand, they should be able to apply. He told me he used analogies because they worked in the same way Jesus Christ used parables. Ed Parker was a religious man and much involved in the Mormon Church.

It's been said that one had to be a Mormon in order to become a senior in the system but I haven't seen evidence of that. Some of the seniors are Mormons but not an inordinate number.

He opened the beginner seminar with the statement "You may hear the same material but in a different way". He was acknowledging that he was going to repeat previous information. But it's the mark of a good instructor that they try to find different ways to present information so that the student understands and integrates the lesson. Learning is defined as a change in behavior. Some add that it results in acquiring a reproducible skill. Take whichever you want or combine them; if you're a teacher you need to know this. He continued by saying, "Anybody can *show* you but if I *share* this with you, you may say I, too, can do it."

Mr. Parker loved to use a chalkboard whenever possible. I've always had a board in my classroom after working with him. It helps students visualize things. Almost every one of the seminars he did in Chicago, he used the board. In this seminar, as in others, he covered the eight considerations, opposites and reverses, point of origin, and other principles that he said were important to him. What I noticed when viewing the tapes is that by this year the beginner and intermediate students were better at correctly answering the questions he asked. I was doing my job.

He was discussing some of the basic principles when he said that he'd taught his four daughters martial arts. (He said martial arts, not Kenpo, which I thought was interesting.) He told them that if they ever had to lift their leg to kick and their dress exposed them he would rather have them red from embarrassment than red from their own blood. I remember him telling me a story about one of the daughters using her skills when she was very young. She had ridden around the block on her bicycle and ran into a hassle with one of the local boys. The boy apparently scared her off and told her not to come back around. Another Parker girl happened to cycle down the same block and ran into the same boy, who thought she was the same girl. Mr. Parker said the girls looked a lot alike. This kid decided to put his hands on her and BAM! she hit him and stopped him cold. Then she got on her bike and calmly rode home. Sounds like a Parker to me.

Bruce Lee was mentioned when he talked about economy of motion. Bruce had been known for his one-inch punch. Parker's point here was that unless you got the desired effect out of a move the short distance of that move's travel made no difference. Rather off-handedly he said that Bruce had lived with him "when he was broke; down and out." He continued with a description of Lee in which he said Bruce Lee was so natural at the arts that you could be a world-class martial artist who had been working on a great kick for years and Bruce would watch you do it, then do it as well as you the first time and better than you the second.

Not breaking the flow of your motion but still getting a desirable effect was a major subject in this seminar. "Once you make a commitment there are several things within that commitment which would not disrupt the action", he stated.

The example was one of using a vertical forearm to strike the outside of the elbow joint to cause a sprain or break. What if the elbow didn't straighten to be broken, what would you do? He showed how the forearm strike could easily be converted into a raking back knuckle with no interruption of the line and flow. This is an important concept in any combat system.

I had asked him to help the students get a handle on how to be explosive in their movements. He went into some depth on breathing and the *kiai,* saying it was important to get the air in you without having to make it an extra move, reminding the class that "and" was the dirtiest word in Kenpo. When he asked what the *kiai* does the answers he got were that it adds power, fortifies and stabilizes the body, and has a psychological effect. One person said it might startle the opponent, and he said, "What if he's deaf?" He granted that it might actually do that, and so would a facial expression,[12] so he said psychological effect would be valid. The *kiai* is used to meld mind and body, which is why one translation of the word is the "spirit shout". I remember that at one seminar when he asked what the *kiai* was

---

[12] What if he's blind?

someone responded with "spiritual screaming". Like they say, it takes all kinds.

To further explain the idea of explosiveness he used an analogy to a stick of dynamite and a fuse. You lit the fuse or trail of gunpowder and waited for the explosion. As technology improved they hooked wires to the TNT and set it off with a plunger, which was faster. He'd watched a James Bond movie the night before and seen 007 use a radio detonator. Click, BOOM! That's the type of immediate explosiveness he wanted.

Articulation of motion was a point he constantly addressed in seminars, using his phonetics of motion analogy. As he spoke about being accurate in your "pronunciation" of movement so as to be "understood" in your application, he related a conversation he had with Julie Andrews. She was married to Blake Edwards,[13] a movie producer who was a student of his. Julie was famous for her acting and singing, particularly how she could sing so fast yet still be understood. When she described the training she had undergone to master the skill, he told her it was the same as what we did with motion. "She was amazed at the parallels", he said, between martial arts and singing. We

---

[13] Edwards had Ed Parker act in two of his *Pink Panther* movies.

must practice and hone our skills in order to enunciate motion, keeping it from being "mumbled", that is, unclear and less effective.

As he would describe the ideas he wanted to embody in a technique he would describe a situation in which you were forced to step forward into the attack even though he said he would prefer that you move back and away to diminish incoming force. In these cases he would refer to Casper, The Friendly Ghost[14] in many seminars when he said that we are unable to walk through a wall like Casper and the situation would mandate a step forward. He used another analogy here for line of action and path of action that I think is useful if the "filled in figure-eight" doesn't work for you. Talking about a sidewalk he said the edges were the lines and the walk itself was the path, with the path being more useful.

"This is so important", he stated, "That you understand the techniques are ideas, not rules." The techniques teach the concepts, principles, methods of motion, and more but they can be changed to adapt as necessary. He told the group, "Don't get depressed if you don't get all your moves in" and proceeded to tell a story to make the point. "A guy

---

[14] Casper was a cartoon character from when I was a kid. Well known then but not now to the younger generation.

came in one day, all depressed. When I asked him what was wrong he told me that he had been the bouncer at a party the night before. He had to ask a man to leave and the guy took a poke at him. So he did the first two moves of *Thundering Hammer* and when he got to the third move the guy was already on the floor. He said, 'I must be getting slow!' And I told him that if the first two moves worked the rest don't apply if the guy's not there."

The opportunity arose to talk about how to use words instead of action to defuse a situation. He told of a few situations in which he used psychology to end a fight before it started. This will give you some insight into the Parker mind. He reminded us that we constantly hear someone making a threat such as "Don't fool with me, I'll kill you", more often on TV and in movies but sometimes in personal conflict situations. Hearing it frequently causes us to become a bit desensitized to the threat. His advice to us was to change the wording to "I'll blind you for life", which would really make one stop and think. He added, "It doesn't work if the guy is already blind", which made the whole room laugh. Another story followed; the Menu of Death, about three men who came into his school and told him they thought they could beat him. "Do you think or do you know?" he asked them and laughed as he told us how they started to consult with one another. "I put doubt in their minds right away". They said they could. He asked them if he could be excused to get a piece of paper and a pencil so that he could take down their names. When they asked if he was going to do that so he could report them he answered no. "When I take your name I want you to tell me how you want to die when I hit you. Do you want to die instantly? Two weeks from now? Or three months?" Their answer was, "You mean we have a choice? We were only kidding", and they left. He concluded by saying that choice of words is important in handling conflict. "If you ask a guy if he's looking for a punch in the mouth, then down to the groin you go" he said. That's classic Parker thinking.

He ended the seminar with recognition of one of the brown belts that had been promoted the night before, getting a fat lip in the process. Taking the positive spin on it Mr. Parker said he should look at it as having more lip to kiss the ladies with. More important was his comment, "I want you to understand where my head is at so you can think like me." In my years of teaching I've told people that the better you can understand him, the better you'll understand the system, and that in turn is one reason why I wrote this book.

England Seminars

Jersey, Channel Islands, 1985

Mr. Parker surprised me when he asked me if I'd like to come along when he was going to Europe to teach. He wasn't providing a free ride but if I paid my airfare the hosts there would take care of accommodations. I jumped at the chance. A few years earlier I had an opportunity to go with an American karate team to Asia for $1500 and didn't take it. I wasn't going to make that type of mistake again.

Arizona's Dennis Conatser and Washington's Skip Hancock went on the trip, too. I went over a few days early to see London then met the rest at Heathrow airport. They had a long layover, so we went to see the Tower of London. I noticed that as we walked through crowds that Mr. Parker had an interesting technique that I surmise was intended to thwart pickpockets. As he walked, he would flutter his hand as it swung back near his wallet pocket.

We flew to Jersey, one of the Channel Islands that are part of the United Kingdom but right off the coast of France, arriving after dark. It was a rough ride and Mr.

Parker asked me what I thought of the landing, since I was a pilot and would become a flight instructor not long after this. "He's either a bad pilot or it's really blowing out there" I said. We got off the plane via air stair and found it was really windy and raining hard. Roy MacDonald and his crew met us. Over the next few days I would meet and work with Graham Lelliott, Roy's number one at the time, who became a long-time friend and eventually my student.

This was a big event, with attendees from Germany, Ireland, and other parts of England. Rainer Schulte, Gary Ellis, Lorcan Carey, Ed Downey, Gino Fuscardi, Jaki McVicar, the late Barney Coleman, Mervyn Ormand, and Diane Wheeler were among those there. These were people who would have an influence on Kenpo in the United Kingdom, Ireland, and Europe not long after and most still do as this is written. The key people in Europe originally were John McSweeney and Rainer Schulte, who brought the art to Ireland and Germany respectively. I'd met Rainer previously at Pasadena, he being the senior IKKA representative for Europe, when he came over for the IKC. Gary Ellis was also with Rainer on that visit.

This really was my first introduction to karate politics on the global level along with my being introduced to the world. I was becoming known largely due to my articles being published in magazines. At this event I would meet people and make acquaintances and friendships that would last years. None of this would have been possible without Ed Parker asking me to come along.

He put all of us to work. We helped out with his classes and he would assign us to certain people he wanted to have extra attention. Our hosts took good care of us, and were receptive and grateful for our being there. This trip created lasting contacts for us all. England's Gary Ellis reintroduced himself to me at the seminar. He likes to tell the story of that meeting. He says I looked at him and said, "You're the guy in the magazine picture". Gary had been in the background of a photo with his teacher at the time, Bob Rose, published years earlier when Gary was a brown belt. He'd gotten his black from Ed Parker in 1980, during the same visit that Graham Lelliott, Dave Williams, and Jim Rennie had earned theirs, so it had been some time. To this day he says he is amazed. I count Eddie Downey among those friends I made on that first trip. I've taught at Ed's school outside Dublin. Years later he would tell me the lessons I taught there "fundamentally changed" their practice. Eddie put me up at a little bed and breakfast there in Celbridge that was a historical place. It was where Mr. Guinness brewed his first pint! Without Mr. Parker's endorsement, who knows if I'd ever had made it over there, met these people, made friends, and been privileged to work with them and their students? This was a rich experience. I saw how he was respected overseas, the depth of his knowledge appreciated, and how he treated his hosts. He truly was a prince and the people loved him.

It was on this trip that I experienced how he used his third person perspective in a discussion situation. Several of us had gone to his hotel to meet him and were sitting in the lobby. Skip, Dennis, and I were there along with some of the European black belts. A discussion was started, the subject generated by a question about majors and minors. It was getting intense as Mr. Parker showed up and sat down, bidding us to continue. I remember watching his face as contributions were made, disputed, questioned, and discussed. You could see the wheels turning and those burning eyes of his went from one person to the next as they spoke. He was absorbed. We had to break it up to leave and I had the chance to ask him what he thought. What struck me was that he said he was fascinated by how people interpreted what he said and how it would factor into discussions. It went back to my first days with him when I would ask him questions based on things I had heard, some of which were rumor or fabrication, and he would say

"They really said that?" as he shook his head. I believe experiences such as this helped him formulate ways to explain a principle or concept that would be less open to being twisted as they were passed down.

Advice to you up and coming practitioners and instructors - if you get the chance to go somewhere with your teacher, strongly consider it.

With the ladies in Jersey.

New England Kenpo

Mid-1980s

Between these other events I was traveling occasionally, starting to do seminars in Ohio and New England. From time to time I'd join Mr. Parker at Steve White's studio in Manchester, New Hampshire or at Tony and Doreen (now DiRienzo) Cogliandro's school in Saugus, Massachusetts. The first time Mr. Parker went to New Hampshire, in 1986, Steve flew me out to be there with them. This was the time when I was getting better known because of all the magazine articles I had written and were published in *Black Belt, Inside Kung-Fu,* and *Karate Illustrated.* Every Kenpo article I wrote was given to Ed Parker first for his approval before it went to the publisher. This insured accuracy and completeness, served as another way for me to increase my knowledge, and helped promote the system. When I'd get an invitation to go somewhere with Mr. Parker or meet him for a seminar, I was always given the nod by him. He would introduce me to people I may not have gotten to meet otherwise and acknowledge me in front of the groups. He was proud of what I was doing for the system. In all the years I studied with Huk Planas, I can remember him doing that only once. Not that I needed a pat on the back but human nature is such that we all like a little recognition. It was much appreciated when I got it from the Grandmaster, and much neglected by Mr. Planas. I'm not saying this to be malicious; I'm saying it to reinforce a basic leadership lesson. You should recognize the achievements of your people.

By arranging to be on the East Coast with Ed Parker I met Remy Presas, the Arnis master. Professor Presas would even call me at my studio in Ft. Myers when he was in Florida after Mr. Parker's passing. Much later I would meet and work with the Professor's students either as staff instructors at a camp somewhere or by invitation to teach in their schools. All this resulted in part from having lunch with him in Boston with Ed Parker.

I also met the late Nick Cerio and his wife Nancy, Don Rodriguez, Greg Silva (who later became known for making or helping make karate schools into successful businesses), and many others who were active in the New England scene. I would eventually teach in studios in New Hampshire, Massachusetts, Rhode Island, and Connecticut. This also allowed me to maintain contact with Joe Palanzo, who was based in Maryland. I'd be invited to his first East Coast camp in 1986, eventually being an instructor at one of his Worldwide Kenpo Karate Association camps years later. It was through his network that when I moved to Florida in 1991, the Kenpo community there would welcome me. Mr. Palanzo and I are friends today. In fact, his daughter married a black belt of one of my black belts. After he started the WKKA, the camp he had been running since 1986 became the WKKA annual camp. He and Huk Planas had been coming to Chicago at my invitation to teach about twice a year each. That gave us a seminar with a senior instructor every three months, and Trejo would come out, too. We picked up on the many aspects of the system quickly this way. Joe Palanzo introduced me to Dr. Myaung Gyi, who would tell me in private conversation later that Ed Parker was the most "out-of-the-box" martial arts thinker he had ever met and called him a genius. Gyi had studied with Gichin Yamaguchi, the Goju–Ryu master, to name but one notable martial artist, so he had good comparisons to make.

Chicago seminars

October 1985

The mat was packed with beginners for the first seminar. He asked how many were there for the first time and was surprised at how many were. In reference to those who had been there before, mostly brown and blacks he said, "They hear me all the time yet they keep coming." He addressed the fact that he had brought the American version of karate here. "Not the Japanese, not the Okinawan, not the Korean version of karate, but the American. What does that mean? It is that which works on the street today." With that, the tone was set for his presentation of his concepts and principles to the beginners.

To illustrate a point about knowing the definition of moves he told a story about a master who was practicing his staff form and his wife came and took the staff away because he kept nicking the ceiling. So he practiced without the staff, doing the movements in the air. When observed by someone who knew nothing about the movements, they were impressed with what he was doing, not knowing that the moves were staff moves, not even empty hand moves. He followed by saying that we could look at someone doing a push-up and say they already had the opponent on the ground and were hitting him with a head-butt. The message in these two stories is that they show how not knowing how to define movement is a problem. "Pronunciation is no good without definition".

In this seminar he would repeat some lessons he had taught me privately, previously introduced in seminars, and published in his books. Point of origin, phonetics of motion, and the importance of knowing opposites and reverses were emphasized yet again. As I watched the videos many years later he was injecting these ideas into his teaching time and again, right up until his passing. Here again he used the term "Polynesian paralysis" when he talked about analyzing reverse motion and telling them about how he was too lazy to rewind a film of himself doing Kenpo and simply hit the reverse switch. He discovered that reverse motion is the other half of motion and integrated it into his system. He also got a bit angry when he described a book he had seen in which the author advocated a technique that had the practitioner jump over a car. "Why not just get out of the way?" he said, "Why jump over? I hate it when people teach others how to get killed! Buy that book and give it to your enemy!" "Logic will give you the answer", he would say.

He said people often insisted to him that there must be one specific way to do a technique. His answer to this was, "How much is 4+4? 6+2? 5+2+1? They all add up to 8, just in a different way." He described how he watched the violin teacher Shinichi Suzuki teach his famed method. Teaching the violin, he'd have them play keeping the violin stationary, then keeping the bow stationary, then moving both to produce the same notes. Today we call it disguised repetition, in which you are actually doing the same thing but in a different manner. This makes the student feel less bored, like they are learning "something new". This too, was integrated into the Parker system, as seen in our techniques.

The story of the 50-cent fan was told to show how one could move the target first and not the blocking hand to avoid the strike. A businessman went to San Francisco and while there decided to buy something for his daughter back home. He selected a beautiful Chinese fan, which he gave to her when he reached home. She used it every day for about a week until it shattered into a hundred pieces. The girl was upset, so he gathered the pieces to take with him on his next trip back to San Francisco's Chinatown. Once there he went back to the shop and asked the owner for a refund. "How much-ee you pay for fan?" the shop owner asked. "It was 50 cents", the man replied. "Ah so. Dollar fan use like this", as he waved the fan in front of his face. "50 cent fan use like this!" as he held the fan without moving it and shook his head from side to side. This story always got laughs and it made the point that the last thing to potentially be hit could be the first thing to move. Move your head, and then (maybe) your hand. He tied in a story about the late karate-man Joe Lewis, who was very strong and fast and Mr. Parker said he liked and respected him. Joe liked to work out with the Parker black belts. His back-knuckle was fast and he kept hitting this one guy with it, who then asked Mr. Parker what he could do about it saying, "Man, he's pretty fast".[15] The advice was, "To beat action, meet it." He showed the man how to oppose the back-knuckle instead of going with it the way he had. Next time he fought Joe he blocked every one of those back-knuckles and had Lewis saying, "Man, I must be getting slow."

There were some young students in the seminar and Mr. Parker interacted with them a lot. He asked them questions,

---

[15] The man was Jack Autry, according to what he said at another seminar.

answered theirs, and used them to demonstrate. He loved kids. When he asked the group as a whole if they were familiar with some principle and didn't get an answer he said, "I feel good I gave you something." That was a big part of his personality.

"Sometimes they ask me if there is anything better than Kenpo. I tell them there are a few superior systems and they go by the names of Smith and Wesson, Remington, and Winchester", he said. He wanted them to know that Kenpo doesn't work for everything, all the time. Other advice he dispensed addressed secret techniques, sequential flow and more on path of action. Regarding secret techniques, he spoke about people who taught in hidden locations. He said they do such things so nobody will know they "don't know nothin'." He followed with "If you can't do it, don't lie your way out."

About sequential flow he said it was something he taught as a back-up method, in case things went wrong, and that's what brought up the gun makers names. Regarding path of action he likened a shin to a knife blade. He didn't like it when tournament rules said a shin kick was not an acceptable scoring tool. It could cut you in half but it's not a point?

Other advice he gave was to look deeper into basics. "Look closer and refine" he said, and went into his standard method of teaching the elements of *Lone Kimono* in the context of the day's lesson (path of action, defensive offense, etc), just as he had with us years ago. He told them to use motion, sometimes emotion in the process of defending themselves, and eliminate commotion. In addition he stated, "Learn motion, how to check leverage points, and moving out of the way."

"I enjoy teaching. I hope we never have to use the art," he said simply. He went on to tell a story about having breakfast with a professional wrestler. They were discussing an incident that had happened the day before in the town they were in. A woman had been raped and 24 witnesses did nothing. He asked the wrestler what he would have done. "Nothing" was the astonishing reply. He asked why, to which the man said that the laws today said since he was a professional fighter he could have been held liable for any damage he may have caused. To prevent being sued by the attacker, he would have chosen not to do anything. He then asked Ed Parker what he would have done. Based on other things you've read earlier you can imagine what he said. "I would have gotten in, did my job, and disappeared!" was his answer.

As he finished his seminar he talked about environment being a critical element in self-defense. He asked the class if they thought it would make a difference if they could get an opponent to take off their jacket and shirt and step outside, if they were in Alaska and it was –60°. "I plant ideas and seeds in your head. You have to go home and pour water on it and make it blossom", he stressed. He told them what he had taught was sophisticated, not complicated.

When I opened the second seminar I introduced Mr. Parker as the coach of the newly formed Budweiser Karate Team, one of the first corporate sponsored karate teams. Joe Palanzo was also a coach, and Frank Trejo was a co-captain, along with Tokey Hill.[16] NFL Films would follow the team at the IKC and make a short documentary on them. In it, David Lee Roth of the rock group Van Halen, would been seen ringside at one of Frank's fights saying, "Frank has a lot of what you would call 'practical experience'".

The mat was not as packed but still full, and we had people from wing chun, other kung-fu styles, and hard styles as well. John McSweeney dropped by, too. Mr. Parker started off with compounding movements and later

---

[16] I wrote an article about the team that was published in the *Karate Illustrated* magazine February 1986 issue.

went into contouring. The examples he used were the common ones he showed most places he went, using *Parting Wings, Five Swords,* and *Leaping Crane* to make his points. Interestingly, he called *Five Swords* the "five-count", using a name that was used many years before when there were few names to techniques.

He re-emphasized many points from the beginner seminar, probably because they were fresh in his mind, but a few commonly taught ones were added. He covered his ideas on relating motion to writing in that we have block, script, and shorthand methods. He compared hard-style movement to block letters in which you stop a line and start another just as you might stop a motion and start another. Kenpo is a flow, like script (or cursive). Shorthand movement combines the block and strike, something we also do in Kenpo.

Making an analogy to speaking he compared some timing to stuttering when one of the participants didn't quite get the flow of the move he was teaching and was breaking up the timing of the moves too much.

"Pair off, and good luck" was a phrase Mr. Parker used frequently when he let the group loose to work on each other. I, and other seniors, think he really meant the "good luck" part, and feel he was referring to whether they would get the idea he was trying to impart or not.

Moving to the subject of contouring, he told the story of a man who came into his school and told him he had studied with a Samoan princess and had an impenetrable defense. The man held his arms up diagonally crossed at the wrists, his hands framing his face at a distance. Mr. Parker first told him his cross was wrong and that it should be on the vertical and horizontal lines. "It's the cross that will mark your grave," he told the man. Obviously the man didn't agree and reset his guard. The Kenpo master shot a punch to the left, causing the man to rock both arms to the left to block. He immediately shot to the right, forcing him to move to that side to block as well. He finished him by shooting a third punch in between the hands, using the man's own contours, which made the man return to the original direction but pulling the incoming hand along with it and into own his face.[17]

He broke down the different methods such as complementary angle, guidelining, tracking, and fitting. He admonished the group to remember that tracking was

---

[17] The Old Man told me at another time that he had rotated his hand palm-out into a finger hook to the eyes as he was pulled in, which had devastating effect.

something that once you used a weapon you left it there to act as a guide for the next weapon, and to consider that the opponent may have that knowledge, too. He had me teach the group a technique called *Dance of Darkness* and used it as the example. Once again, he demonstrated leadership skills by having one of his people teach and thereby showcasing them a bit. He did this in many venues with positive results.

Mr. Parker urged the group to think about how many ways they could follow the body contours, both theirs and the opponent's, and how they could break the contours by complementing them instead of opposing them. He demonstrated how with a volunteer and then had the group practice. When I watched the video it was amazing just how many did not get the idea. They opposed the bodylines instead, over and over, totally missing the point. When I taught seminars myself over the years I'd see the same phenomena. You'd explain something, ask if they understood, get the affirmative answer, and then have them pair up. Almost always the people would go back to doing what they were doing before the explanation. A definition of learning is a change in behavior. Based on that, did they learn it?

Following contours in a variety of manners essentially means using your contours or the opponent's. You could, of course, use environmental contours but that's getting away from where we are now. When Ed Parker taught us that "For every move, concept, principle, or definition, there is an opposite and a reverse", he gave us important keys. You can follow a contour. Yet, you can also change a contour. Human bodies are flexible and in martial arts we constantly change the shape of our body as we move through time and space. Could we not modify our shape at a given time to change its contour? It is the thinking that there is an opposite and a reverse that led me to this discovery, and I found that practice used in the Russian art of Systema. We DO modify shape when we step sideways and block, making ourselves a narrow target (the third consideration of combat). That's one practice of the idea. There are others, and I teach this idea today in my classes and seminars.

We had a guest at the seminar he would talk to while the group was working, and that person was off-camera but next to it. As I watched the video I was able to eavesdrop on what he was saying to him. Mr. Parker was talking about his knife concepts since so much of his blade work was based on contouring. At that point he was joined by Al McLuckie, a *guro* in Serrada Eskrima from Ft. Wayne, Indiana. Ed Parker later told me he thought Al was above average in his skills and the man he was speaking with was told that he had watched Al work and thought he was very good. They briefly talked about the stick and knife systems and Mr. Parker said he used to "spy on the Filipino guys" and watch their movements. He mentioned that he had introduced Ben Largusa to the world at the 1964 IKC, the same event Bruce Lee did his first big demo at. The audio is not very clear and there were parts I missed due to background noise but how fortunate I was to have him allow me to tape these sessions. It was like the moviemakers' slogan from a while back, "See it again for the first time!"

Grafted principles were next. He used a "Victim; I mean volunteer" to show how to change from one method of execution to another. Jim Lowell was the victim of his demonstrations of changing from a thrust to a lift and a hammer to a thrust. Jim said, "To feel is to believe". Parker's ideas on changing a punch to a lifting forearm or a hammerfist to an uppercut are, in his words, "A time-saver and a rib-breaker."

He was elaborating on weapon ranges and how to use the upside and downside of the paths to do the job. This led to a discussion of line versus path and how perspective dictates how you see the shapes involved. A square viewed at an angle is a diamond. The path or orbit makes a difference and the changes were defined as being switches or adjustments, with the adjustment being the lesser in degree. He tied all this together; the path and line of action, orbital switch or adjustment, and change of weapon range with a few quick moves to illustrate. He shot a punch, the man moved; he changed to a forearm and altered the path as he used a type of upward elbow. Brilliant stuff. "I know it works; I tried it on my mother-in-law" he joked. He blended an example of affecting the man's timing by ½ and ¼ beat by using a forearm with a back-knuckle, dropping it down instead of retracting it. "What do they do when you pull it back?" he asked. The answer is they fill the space. To prevent that, he used the forearm and forced the opponent back beyond their point of origin to keep them behind the action.

The Universal Pattern was brought up again as part of this discussion. In a question directed at me he asked, "Why did I name it the Universal pattern, Lee?" Before I could answer he said, "If you study the structure of our solar system down to the structure of an atom, is it not almost the same?" It was not the content he was pointing out, it was the fact that the structure is similar from largest to smallest, just as in the moves of Kenpo. Again, your point of view is what makes it work. He commented that you can be inside the pattern, outside it, part of it, or superimposed on it. This sort of abstract thinking tended to lose some people when he taught.

As he was finishing his seminar he asked if anyone had questions. A few questions were asked and one was rather picky. "Don't get technical on me" he said, and immediately fired a question back, which was, "What's a grab?" There was no answer. "The after-move of a catch. I've thought about these things." His point was made. He had vocabulary and terminology for the masses but there was even more that he had and was in the process of formalizing and would later publish. He was looking forward to volumes Four and Five of *Infinite Insights* to come out and cause us to wrack our brains. "People won't make fun of us because we have concepts and principles that they haven't even thought of yet", he said. That's an interesting comment.

In a nod to the people from other systems in attendance he finished with this statement; "I'm not trying to make you a Kenpo stylist. I just want to enhance what you do." As he bowed us out he said, "It's always a pleasure to come to Chicago."

Australia visit

Sydney, 1986

Frank Trejo, Dennis Conatser, and I went with Ed Parker to Sydney, Australia. I have part of this trip on video, courtesy of Dennis. It has three demos on it, including the demo we did at a tournament, the focal point of the trip. Mr. Parker narrated it while the three of us worked each other over. It was great fun, as demonstrating with Frank always is. Frank was the senior on this trip and he was the star of the show. His skills are excellent and he injected his sense of humor into the demo. We finished with a two-man attack scenario that ended with Dennis suffering a groin grab and Frank throwing two paper balls he had hidden in his *gi* into the air on the pull-out. The crowded gymnasium roared and clapped as we bowed out.

Once again, I saw how Ed Parker was respected, now on the opposite side of the world. Our host, John Van Wyk, had arranged everything to help promote Parker Kenpo "Down-Under". His right-hand man was Mike "Mick" Crim, a Hapkido 4th dan who was switching to Kenpo. Mick is a real people person and we keep in touch today. In the late 90s he would phone me and tell me one of his students would be coming to Florida to visit but wasn't sure when. Two weeks later a man showed up at my studio, suitcase in hand and a tough-guy attitude. Jack Nilon was Mick's black belt and a pretty good one at that. Jack eventually came to Florida to train for six months and became integrated into the studio. We were sad to see him go back home. I tell you this because it's an example of how treating people right reaps benefits, and not just for you. Jack returned for another year and is still teaching.

Our schedule there was hectic for a short visit of five days. We were well treated here, too. While we did have a rather heavy teaching schedule coupled with the demos, and a tournament, we did get to do a little sightseeing in downtown Sydney. Mick made sure of that.

One morning Mr. Parker was being interviewed on television, the show was *Good Morning, Australia*. Frank was in the background doing forms under some pine trees as they asked Mr. Parker about Kenpo and Elvis. Dennis and I were back at the hotel watching the television. Frank broke out of the combination of forms he was doing and did some interesting movements two or three times that involved him going into a crane stance as he slapped the bottom of his foot with his opposite hand. Then he went back to the form. When he got back to the hotel I asked him what he was doing there. His reply was that he had gotten a pine needle stuck in his foot and was trying to get it out without having to break the action since it was live TV.

We wrapped the trip with the tournament. I competed in black belt forms and took first place, but gave the trophy to the second place winner as a goodwill gesture and was rewarded with applause from the crowd. I would find out next year when we returned that John was not happy about that at all. He apparently wanted the Kenpo people to take as many of the trophies as possible. *C'est la vie.* Mr. Parker told me after the division was over that he had watched me work. He laughed and said the other competitors watched intently at first, then they hung their heads as I blew them away. "They'd never seen anything like that before", was his comment.

On departure, John, Mick, Greg and some others saw us off. We flew to Hawaii for a few days on Oahu. Frank and I bunked up at a Waikiki Beach hotel Mr. Parker had arranged for us. Dennis joined his wife there and the Old Man stayed at the house he had there that his daughter, Darlene, lived in with her husband and child. Trejo and I went a little nuts on the Waikiki strip, the Conatsers went sightseeing, and Mr. Parker stayed with his family. He took us down to Hanauma Bay, where some of us went snorkeling. I have a picture of him, standing with Dennis Conatser, and overlooking the ocean, next page. I had to wonder what he was thinking but I feel he was really enjoying being home. He told us stories of bringing Elvis to Hawaii, and about what it was like when he was a kid. It was pretty cool to be in Hawaii with Ed Parker.

One particularly memorable thing was how he took us to the Polynesian Cultural Center there on Oahu. The Center is owned by Brigham Young University and many of the college kids from the South Pacific islands work there while attending school. I remember that Leilani had flown over to meet him and she was with us at the Center that day. The PCC showcases the various cultures found in the South Pacific in a variety of ways and attracts a lot of visitors. Frank Trejo took the picture below, and that's me clowning with a tiki there.

We saw the Samoan fire dance, the Hawaiian hula, and walked through the recreations of island villages from Fiji, New Zealand, and Tonga. Frank and I were extremely fortunate to happen on an actual ceremony when visiting Maoris approached the Maori village there. The villages at PCC are actual "working" villages, not simple recreations with people dressed up like islanders. The leader of the visiting group performed the traditional approach and greeting as the residents' chief responded in kind. It was a challenge and response ceremony, with the visitor shouting in their native language, gesturing toward his people, and waving a large stick that doubled as his cane and being answered likewise. Frank and I observed afterward that the whole thing was much like how street kids handled entries to their turf, both of us having grown up in big cities. Once again, Ed Parker provided us a lesson in the workings of a larger world.

Big Four Seminar

Chicago, September 1986

I put together a big event in Chicago and flew in Ed Parker, Frank Trejo, Joe Palanzo, and Huk Planas as the instructors. This combination had never been done before.[18] We had people from ten states spread across the country there. My studio was packed. Ed Parker's opening statements included, "I'd like to thank Lee Wedlake for his ability to bring us together. It was a nice acknowledgment. The evening before the event we had a test at my school and Huk, Frank, Joe, and Ed Parker kicked me to fifth degree black. All of them had a hand in my maturing as a practitioner and instructor, and I thank them for that.

Huk taught forms, Mr. Palanzo did techniques, and Mr. Trejo covered freestyle applications.[19] (This was when the Budweiser Karate Team was going strong and Mr. Parker,

---

[18] It was the first time the four had taught together.
[19] Frank had just been on the cover of *Karate and Kung-Fu Illustrated* magazine with Mr. Parker, the September 1986 issue, getting clawed. It was the first of a three-part series on the system.

Frank and Joe were involved in it. Frank and Joe wore their embroidered team uniforms.)

Photo by Brad Crooks.

It was almost as if there was an unspoken competition between the teachers and Mr. Parker blew everyone away with his seminar. "Come on up here, we're gonna have a good time," he said as he waved the participants in closer to him. He meant it and he wanted everyone to enjoy what he had to share. He then made some introductions. Dennis Conatser was present from Arizona, Arthur Smith was there, writing for *Black Belt* magazine, and Jim Thompson came up from Tennessee. Mr. Parker said that he had three "animals" that he had spike collars for, with the spikes on the inside so he could control them. He said they were Tino Tuliosega, Leonard Mao, and Jim Thompson.[20] John McSweeney and Gil Hibben were there, too.

He told the group they would see the "spectrum of Kenpo" in that class and proceeded to begin with his Eight Considerations of Combat. Time was spent on environment, that being what is around you, on you, and in you. His descriptions of how it worked in both positive and negative ways were interesting. What's around you and on you is largely self-explanatory. However, what's in you could be what you ate, whether you are ill, or even so excited you are convinced you can beat the world. He explained in depth how they built upon each other as he questioned the group about the priority he had designed with them. This led to his analogy of the mechanic and engineer of motion so many of us have been introduced to. He explained that, as a mechanic, you could take something apart and put it back together in working order. As an engineer you can design the parts to be used in the process.

---

[20] He stated in front of everyone that Mao had beaten a man so badly once they had to amputate the man's arm.

He wanted us to be engineers of motion. He himself, was often referred to as the "Magician of Motion".[21]

As he began to talk about how to break down a technique he asked the group to select one to discuss. Wouldn't you know it was *Five Swords* again! People would complain that Ed Parker taught the same thing a lot but when the group asked for that again, you have to wonder. He analyzed each movement, highlighting principles of body momentum, checking, the ghost image concept, lines of entry, delivery, and methods of execution. He'd query the class, get an answer and then ask them if they thought the answer was right (even if it was) and said, "I'm always gonna put some doubt in your mind!" This is something I have found to be a valuable life lesson; Challenge what you are told is true.

He touched on the three points of view, again emphasizing how important it was to look at things from more than one perspective. He also pointed out common problems, reasons for them, and offered solutions. People were doing heel-palms and chops with thumbs sticking out, so he showed them what could happen as far as damaging

---

[21] The July 1979 issue of *Black Belt* magazine's cover says "The Magician of Motion Reveals the Secrets of His Art". This is the issue in which he names protégés. This was the first of a three-part series.

themselves but also how they could increase their effectiveness by doing it right. He called the fingers and thumb a family and admonished them to "keep the family together". Family is highly important to the Hawaiians and Ed Parker was no exception. They call it *Ohana*. Some had a problem with the rear hand check on the opening move so he suggested reverting back to childhood and stuck his thumb in his mouth to keep the hand high, which got a laugh. When he got people to see that much of what we do was so simple, he said they'd get a slanted forehead when they had this realization, slapping himself in the head as people do when they discover something simple.

I found it interesting in retrospect that one of the points he made on *Five Swords* about not over-rotating on the last move as so many people do, is still today a fairly common mistake. "Over-rotation splits the force and changes the lines", he said. All too often students of Kenpo do exactly that type of over-rotation in many techniques and it causes them to either miss, glance off, or lose power. I saw a video online of an instructor from the Tampa area, who had never met Ed Parker, showing exactly that mistake as he taught and demonstrated. He even stated that he thought over-rotation was "What Ed Parker had in mind when he created the technique". I'd have laughed if it weren't making me sick.

A "volunteer" was grabbed out of the front row and Mr. Parker explained how you could prefix, suffix, insert, alter (weapon and/or target), regulate (speed, force, or both), rearrange, or delete movements using a base move. The beginner freestyle technique *B1a* was used as the vehicle to transmit this information. In my humble opinion I think those standard freestyle techniques are great for doing just that and there are not enough schools teaching them. My former teacher, Huk Planas, said freestyle should be freestyle (no patterns) and therefore the standard freestyle techniques were not necessary. I disagreed, and still do. If you teach a student to spar you still need to arm them with something before they get in there. I've seen too many students say, "What do I do?" Giving them simple 1-2 or 1-2-3 moves like these is highly beneficial. The freestyle techniques are part of the system and should be taught.[22] As he described how we did an alphabet of motion he talked about an allegorical man who said he didn't use the letter X very often and wanted it taken out of his alphabet. He

---

[22] Some people teach the system without giving instruction in the basics either. It's like teaching the letters of the alphabet as you teach a student to write words or sentences, instead of beforehand.

reminded the class that now he had an incomplete alphabet. What would that man do if he needed an X? And like certain movements in Kenpo, what would we do if they were taken out only for the reason that they were infrequently used? We'd have an incomplete alphabet of motion.

He finished his seminar with family related movements within the techniques and how reactionary positions were so important. As he did one technique the crowd broke out in applause. That's a great reaction to get in a seminar, and not all that common. When he described Dimensional Stages of Action he said Kenpo works all the ranges, out-of-range, in-range, contact penetration, and contact manipulation (and maintenance), which allowed one to work in any situation. Using *Aikido* as an example he stated, "They go from Phase One to Phase Four without working in between", he observed, adding that he had nothing against the system. A question was asked about handling wrestlers. This was before the advent of mixed martial arts as they are known today but signs of the upcoming trend were in place. He briefly commented that spins and maneuvers to displace their weight and balance were what were needed. I can only speculate what he might have developed if he had lived to see what was being done with mixed martial arts today. His experience as a judo man and with grappling arts affected Kenpo as it is today; which is itself a form of mixed martial art. He always looked to develop answers to situations based on common sense, grounded in logic and principle. Today's martial arts environment would have been fertile ground for the Parker mind, and is for others in our system today.

Mr. Parker was also included on an in-joke for one of the people there. Tom McLennan is a notorious collector of things Kenpo, like a lot of people.

Author (Lee Wedlake), Ed Parker and Tom McLennan

He could make a pest of himself, constantly asking the Old Man all sorts of questions, but Mr. Parker treated him rather like a son. Pete Tomaino and I asked him to present Tom with a special Kenpo item for his collection at the seminar. We had Kenpo Karate bumper stickers with an IKKA crest with "The Ultimate in Self-Defense" on them. We wrapped one around a roll of toilet paper. As part of the opening of the seminar he announced we had a special gift for Tom. Then he pulled it out of the bag, and presented it to him as he said, "Tom always has questions, so I tell him to write them down on toilet paper and tear them off as they get filled. But we know he won't use it out of respect for the patch". The crowd roared, Mr. Parker gave him a big hug, and Tom took it as a good sport.

It was Huk's 40th birthday. Coincidentally as he, Mr. Parker, and I were driving down the Tri-State Tollway from O'Hare airport we saw a car with a bumper sticker that said "40 isn't old - if you're a tree". That Saturday night after the seminars, we had a party in a suite at a local hotel. Every time someone new entered the room everyone sang Happy Birthday again. The party got a little loud and someone sent security up to ask us to be quieter, "Or they'd have to ask us to leave". That got quite laugh from the partying karate people but they toned it down. Mr. Parker was in the bedroom side of the suite watching a Rambo movie with Gil and a few other guys; appropriate, since Gil made the knives for one of the movies.

Second Australia visit

Australia, 1987

For this trip we had a team of 13 people from all over the U.S. I was the team captain this trip, being the senior rank. Mr. Parker put me in charge of creating a demo team for the duration. Spokane's Skip Hancock was there and was working a lot of live-blade stuff on the trip. America's East and West coasts were represented, as was the Midwest. Mrs. Parker and daughter Sheri came along, too.

On the flight over he sat with Skip Hancock and myself and we discussed some of the new terminology he and Skip had been working on. Skip had made himself available to Mr. Parker to help get the *Infinite Insights* later volumes out, to the extent that Skip was staying at the Parker house and he and Edmund Jr. were slaving away on the books in some upstairs rooms. Skip showed me some of the work he was doing on a new version of the *Accumulative Journal*. We were awake at 4AM due to the time change and got to talking about what he was working on. I remember disagreeing with some of what he was doing and he slammed his book shut in frustration and went off to his room.[23]

Coincidentally, General Chuck Yeager, the man who broke the sound barrier, was on the plane to Sydney with us but he was first off and long gone, so we didn't get a chance to meet him[24]. Our group came out of baggage claim to a sizable crowd there to greet us and some were from other systems, too. The walkway out to the parking lot was lined on both sides with students in *gi*, standing in meditation horse stances and saluting us. That was a nice gesture, but a bit much for a guy like me, though I appreciated it. That's Skip Hancock in the photo from my collection.

---

[23] When Skip originally came to Pasadena I was told by Frank Trejo to work with him. He was looking for audience with Mr. Parker. When I spoke with Mr. Parker about Skip he told me to make the decision as to whether or not to bring him along to the house when I went over for my private lesson. I didn't see any harm and I took Skip with me. The rest is history.

[24] On the trip home from the first visit the pilot made an announcement in the middle of the night over the South Pacific that we could see Halley's comet crossing the sky. I'd never seen one before or since. And nobody will see this one until 2061.

We got to our accommodations, the bulk of the team at a motel and Skip, myself, and the Parkers at John's new house. At the motel they had a small bus we would be traveling in that had a sign on the outside saying the U.S. Karate Champions were on board, along with the sponsors name. That bus would take us to and from the gym we practiced at for the demos, the seminar locations, demo locations, sightseeing, and the tournament. The Aussies arranged a visit to a zoo where we could see the wallabies and hold a koala bear. A trip to the Blue Mountains was on the schedule and that's where the group shot you may have seen in Leilani Parker's book, *Memories of Ed Parker*, was taken.

We did several demos to promote John's clubs. One was at a big shopping mall. Everyone was in on the action. Mick Crim did self-defense. Skip demonstrated the knife, the Tostens, Welthas, and Ohio's Lou Laird with David Sites did their stuff. Mr. Parker was our emcee and Skip and I brought him in our demo in the role of Big Daddy, who chastised us for having numerous weapons hidden in our uniforms by hauling us away by the ears.

Disarming me.

Skip and I being led away by the ears.

A cherished memory I have of this evening is that when I ran Form Five on the stage, he was behind me and I could hear him say, "Go, Lee, Go!".

This was the trip where a riot broke out at the tournament. I've told the story on YouTube and gotten responses that verify it happened as I remember.

Mr. Parker and I were ringside for heavyweight black belt sparring. Lou Laird had beaten his opponent in fighting. While the competitor was not upset, having lost fairly, his instructor was quite agitated and indicated to his student not to shake Lou's extended hand. Lou looked at Mr. Parker and shrugged. The ring corners were marked with small orange cones and the instructor kicked one into the ring, hitting Lou in the chest. Lou looked at again at Mr. Parker, who shook his finger "no". Lou took no action and said nothing about the insult.

The student and instructor stormed down the aisle away from the ring amidst hundreds of spectators whose folding chairs had been arranged around that one black belt competition ring. By now the student was as agitated as the instructor, who was screaming about how they "Hadn't come here to be cheated by these f*****g Americans". He then picked up a chair and threw it into the crowd as spectators surged out of their seats and away from the action. The chair hit one of the members of Ernesto Presas' Arnis club. (Ernesto is Professor Remy Presas' younger brother.) All the Filipinos stood up and the fight was on. I saw one man standing on a chair and clubbing combatants on their heads. One of the karate fighters was yelling as his scalp was split open and blood ran down his face, yet wanting to fight some more.

I grabbed Mr. Parker by his belt and pulled him next to me. My thinking was that if any one of the Arnis guys had a knife and lost it, it was possible someone in the crowd that was swirling around might try to stick him. He said, "I'll stay right here" and I moved off to secure Sheri and Mrs. Parker. I had enough team members and Aussies to set up a sort of perimeter to get the Parkers out a side door to our bus. The place was up for grabs and the police showed up. It calmed for a minute as rioters moved out the gym door into the hallway. Something re-ignited the fight and people started spilling back into the gym with fists flying.

The police were surrounding the building as we got everyone into the bus and pulled away. I was amazed at how fast that many cops got there. Nobody in our group got hit but Mr. Parker was asking if we had seen how this guy moved and that guy did this or that. When I had grabbed his belt and pulled him back a bit to secure his position he was intent on the action, which was like a laboratory to him.

There was speculation the next day that it may have been planned by a particular group, a set-up to make John look bad as the promoter and a figure in Australian Kenpo. It made news in town.

We found out that the tournament had been advertised as a U.S. versus Australia event and that there was to be a team fight that we had not been told about. I have the flyer. Later, I was told that as we did our demos the days before the tournament that the registered team fighters pulled out after seeing what we were doing. I'd like to believe that but the Aussies I know would prefer to take a chunk out of you than cancel out. Like Mr. Parker said in a television interview that week, 'The Australians love to hit and be hit.'" There was no team fight because it was cancelled when nobody showed to fight. Why nobody showed is unknown to me.

I have been back to teach in Australia since then, as have some of those who went over back then and several other instructors. Graham Lelliott has often been down there too, and some of the Aussies have come to attend his bi-annual Wonder Valley camp in California. I attribute this cross-traffic back to those visits by Ed Parker in the 80s.

The Late 1980s

In 1988 I closed my studio on Southwest Highway in Oak Lawn and ran classes at a racquet club. I was now working full-time as a flight instructor because the karate business had gone bad across many parts of the country and I wanted out of a commercial school. While I had been working on my pilot certificates and ratings Mr. Parker had expressed to me that he always wanted to learn to fly. He enjoyed flying around with Elvis and would hang out near the cockpit during the flights, talking with the pilots. He'd have been a good pilot because flying is so three-dimensional and he'd have grasped that quickly.

This was the period I stopped going to the Internationals due to my work schedule, and the semi-annual visits were curtailed because we didn't really have a place or student numbers to support a seminar. My contact with him was by phone and the occasional time when I could meet up with him at a seminar "back East."

I continued to write for the magazines and would do so even after he passed away. The main event in that this period for me was the Tribute to Ed Parker held at the Bonaventure Hotel in downtown Los Angeles in 1988.

The Tribute was the brainchild of Tom Bleecker, a longtime Kenpo man with a school in Solvang, CA. The event was a banquet, attended by hundreds. I went out a few days early and met with Barbara Hale, who was integral to making it happen, and the West LA crew. Somehow I wound up as part of the team that set up the event at the hotel and I ran the audio-visual for the tribute. This was the weekend Tom Bleecker would meet Linda Lee, the late Bruce Lee's wife. He'd later marry her and they'd eventually divorce.

What a show it was! The whole family was there, even Ed Parker's mother, who'd been flown in from Hawaii. She was a tiny little thing and close to 90 years old at the time. How she handled those big Parker boys was a tribute in itself. As he entered the room the Emerson, Lake, and Palmer piece entitled *Fanfare for a Common Man* was played. A special video showcasing his life was shown, with pictures from childhood to the present. Many a testimony was made; Skip Hancock's team demonstrated, hula girls danced, and Ed Parker played his ukulele. When he spoke to the crowd he wore a traditional Hawaiian male-style lei. He had tears in his eyes and choked up when he said he wished his father could have been there to see what he had become. Chuck Norris was there at his table with him, and most of the seniors in the system were present at the event. It truly was an event to attend and done at the right time. Who knew he had less than two years to live?

I was in the car with him on the way down to the West Los Angeles studio. The Santa Monica location had been closed and the studio relocated to WLA. Larry Tatum had been removed from the manager position and others were filling in. On the way down Mr. Parker told me that he would soon want to have me and a few others take his place when he couldn't make it to do a seminar. I was surprised to hear him say that but grinning on the inside. Here I met John Sepulveda for the first time. John would later become one of the foremost instructors in the system and a respected senior. His people stood out in the belt test to be held that evening before the Tribute. Actor Jeff Speakman, of the movie *The Perfect Weapon*, was taking his test for third degree black at the West Los Angeles studio. It was a large group testing and a group just as large sitting on the exam board. (That would commonly happen. When the word got out there was going to be a test, people would come out of the woodwork to be there, some hoping to get bumped up. You'd hear him say someone was "in it" rather than "at it" for a number of years and wouldn't be promoted. Yet others would be moved up at a test in consideration of rank, time in grade, and contribution to the art.) Mr. Parker and I were getting into our *gis* when he said, referring to Speakman, "This kid is on the verge of making it, he's going to be a star." "Do we still have to promote him?" was my rather smart-ass answer. Jeff wore a *gi* that was full of holes. To me, it was disrespectful. That evening Mr. Parker and I would butt heads about the decision to promote applicants, at one point almost nose to nose. I was not happy with the results of the test and said so. That kicked off a two-hour discussion that resulted in everyone being promoted anyway. I went back to Chicago feeling angry. But that's me and that's how I get from time to time. I don't think rank should be given away. I felt that way about some of those people at that time, right or wrong. But it's something I think many martial artists deal with somewhere along the line.

The Last Chicago Seminar

November 1990

I asked my people if they were coming to the Ed Parker seminar in mid-November. "I'll catch him next time", "Can't afford this one", or even "He always does the same stuff, anyway" were answers I got. Attendance was not bad; Steve Hatfield brought some of his people all the way from Ohio, and others from Pennsylvania, Wisconsin, and other parts of Illinois attended. Mr. Parker talked about Jeff Speakman and his upcoming movie, *The Perfect Weapon*. He was excited about it and told stories about how he was working on the set. It would showcase Kenpo, his life's work. He said as he pointed to his crest patch, "You'll see this on the screen." Going on the road to promote the movie with Jeff in the coming March was something he was looking forward to.

I introduced him as being from Pasadena and he corrected me by saying to the group, "My body rests in Pasadena but my heart is in Hawaii." Little did we know that in just over a month, his body would literally rest in

Glendale, California. He would suffer a fatal heart attack in the Honolulu airport on a trip home to see his mother.

He opened the seminar by saying that what he was teaching was not difficult and that he wanted to get you to know <u>how</u> to think, not <u>what</u> to think, something my dad had said when I went to college. "If someone tells you that you have to do something a certain way, here's what I tell you to do. Find the nearest exit and leave", he said as he pointed to the door. With this as the premise of the seminar he proceeded to teach us about his Dimensional Stages of Action, the rearrangement concept, and variable expansion.

When describing the four stages of action, he compared them to other systems. In one, he said, "They await contact while we create contact". He used the basic beginner freestyle techniques (B1a, etc) to make his points about the height, width, and depth zones, timing, and use of the opposite side. Cancellation of the zones is critical and he demonstrated the applications and possible counters when done incorrectly. He used the example of Lawrence Welk, a bandleader popular many years ago that was famous for his "one and a two" count. Mr. Parker said he didn't want that type of timing because there is a big difference between "and" and "with". He wanted the grab with the punch, not a grab and then a punch. Throughout he had the participants switch to the opposite side to work the movements while stressing that doing so would help them to become more versatile in their responses.

He made an interesting statement about the B3a maneuver, saying it was made simpler for beginners, adding that you should really grab and punch with the crossover instead of punching with the step out.

"Once you learn the basics, can't you multiply action?" he asked. This led into the Formulation Stage lesson in which he once again showed how to prefix, suffix, alter, rearrange, and delete. While altering he described how one could adjust the weapon, target, or both and by adjusting the weapon it altered timing, power, and speed. He followed this with an important statement that knowing all this "Creates an ideal technique". With this knowledge one would then use the rearrangement concept, the "Four Factorial" and Variable Expansion.

"The rearrangement concept is interesting and very sophisticated," he said and defined sophisticated as being compounded simplicity. By using his Four Factorial example of an inward block, outward chop, inward elbow, and back hammerfist, he showed how those four moves could be made into 24 sequences. Try it. The Variable Expansion aspect applies when you re-define each of those movements and change the weapons, applications and zones. The idea is to examine and exhaust the possibilities of each to increase your knowledge and ability. He would use the inward block against the inside of a right punch, the chop to the neck, the inward elbow to the jaw hinge and the hammerfist to the groin. If you redefine the chop and use it as an extended outward block inside a left punch, you can use the inward block as a rake to the bridge of the nose, then elbow the head and strike the groin. Changing the chop to a whip, hammerfist, heel-palm, etc. are other examples. Using the hammerfist as a downward block, then blocking the left with the outward chop and going on are further examples. Variable Expansion from a specific point looks to see what else can be accomplished. Much of this was not "new" to us but reinforcement is always valuable. While he would often repeat information, sometimes a question would trigger something he hadn't addressed with us before, or he'd tell another related story to keep the troops engaged. One point made here was that we needed to find a way to get the ideas across to people with such varied backgrounds. He said you could describe it one way using terms such as Line of Action and Path of Action and it would make sense to an engineer. Use terms such as upper case and lower case and it makes sense to an English major.

Liken it to a squeegee and a window washer gets it. The terminology of Kenpo was designed to get us on the same page.

He promoted me to sixth degree black that day, the last promotion I would earn from him. I have that diploma on my wall next to a portrait Ed Jr. gave me on my 50th birthday. The portrait shows his dad in a white *gi*, which is rather unusual.

He worked on Form Seven with me that weekend and I recall him moving well. He was fast, powerful and I remarked to him that he was looking good. I honestly hadn't seen him moving like that in a while and he hadn't been looking good prior to that. In fact, the night before the seminar at the dinner table he sat with his eyes closed and trembled. I asked him if he was OK and he said he just wanted a minute. He soon opened his eyes and almost jumped up from the table, ready to go. I often wonder of he had a small-scale heart attack there at the table. Later, and the next day, he seemed fine.

Pre-dawn phone call

December 16, 1990

My phone rang in the early morning, which is usually never good. It was Edmund saying, "I am calling my father's friends to let them know he passed away yesterday." He briefly gave me the details, then I thanked him and hung up, stunned. This was the second instructor I'd lost and it was a sudden occurrence with both. I believe we grieve, to a degree, out of selfishness. But I also believe we grieve for the greater losses, those losses that are realized when we see that that person won't be around to nurture not only us but family, friends and make contributions to society. It's mitigated for many by the thought or belief that things are better for the one we lost and we are happy for them. I felt bad for his family and church for their loss, too. I was sad, and I couldn't face my class to tell them Mr. Parker had passed without choking up. I missed him, and still do. That's the selfish part of me wanting him to be here so I could ask questions and have him as part of my life as I was a small part of his. I have a sense of loss because we don't have his genius to continue actively contributing to martial arts knowledge.

The funeral

We do what human beings have done for ages – we carry on. I, and others, keep the flame of Kenpo knowledge burning by teaching. Over two thousand people showed up for his funeral. I was fortunate to have Leilani Parker see me when I arrived at the church and allow me a few minutes alone with him before hundreds of others were let in. I had a good relationship with the Parker family over the years and maintained it. Leilani was always cheerful when I spoke to her in the years after his death and I regret not having seen her in the months between when she was diagnosed with pancreatic cancer and her passing.

Inside the church, the Mormon Temple in Pasadena, they had to open the dividers and find hundreds more chairs to accommodate the throng. I really don't know if people were standing outside as well, although it seemed so. There were words from friends, students, and family members but the most powerful memory I have from the ceremony was that of Edmund Jr. He spoke sincerely yet also made us laugh, however what really left the impression I have was what he did as his father's casket was taken from the church. There is a well known, if not famous, song written by the last reigning queen of Hawaii, Lilioukailani, named *Aloha 'Oe*. The words of the chorus are:

Farewell to you,
Farewell to you,
The charming one who dwells in the shaded bowers.
One fond embrace,
'Ere I depart,
Until we meet again.

Edmund and others sang this song, but Edmund sang it *to* his father, not just *for* his father. He leaned forward from the pulpit, an arm extended with his hand open in the body language of letting go and sending off. The image stays with me and I can hear the voices singing that song that will forever remind me of the day my teacher was buried.

They had to close the freeway between Pasadena and the Glendale cemetery and have a police escort. Hundreds of Kenpo instructors were at the gravesite. I saw Huk Planas and Danny Insosanto with their arms around each other and crying their eyes out. The list of practitioners of many arts there that day would be too long to list here. What was striking was that so many people had flown in at a time just before Christmas, making it more difficult to make it, but there they were. Steve Hatfield had driven to Chicago's O'Hare airport from Columbus, Ohio in a snowstorm to make the flight with me and some other Chicago people. Steve later asked me whom I was surprised to see there. My answer was that I was surprised to see him there. You'd expect the seniors and people from other arts, so many of who had gotten a career boost through an association with Ed Parker. But guys like Steve, from a small town outside Columbus, driving through the snow and enduring delays and a long flight before a major holiday shows just how deeply Ed Parker affected people. It's a privilege to be associated with people like him.

Conclusion

By reading this you've been able to follow a progressive timeline of the experiences my students and I had with one of the geniuses of martial arts. You've read his words, principles, analogies, and stories as told to others and myself. The crucial elements of Kenpo were stressed time and again in my private lessons and the seminars. You also saw how I was started with the basics and worked my way up through the system and that the progression of the seminars was done the same way. There wasn't much point in bringing him out to Chicago to teach Form Six when we didn't have a good grounding in the principles and methods of motion in the Parker system. I (we) had to adapt, adopt, and ingrain to grow into what we are today.

After he passed away I kept up my training with Richard "Huk" Planas and continued in the same manner. We worked on basics, then went through the system several times, refining and detailing. Back to basics and then more work, for 20 more years. Anyone who works or worked with Huk recognizes the pattern. The advanced material is not much use if the basics are weak, a message Ed Parker pounded in.

While I strongly believe in reinforcing the basics, a steady diet of that kills the interest of most. I try to keep it interesting because that's what worked for me. Kenpo has kept me mentally stimulated for 50 years. My interest in other arts has always brought me back to Kenpo by making me realize the keys are in our system and you truly do have to think about what we have and what we are doing, just as he said so many times. He used to say that life insurance pays the beneficiaries, while you pay the premiums. With Kenpo, he said, you pay the premiums but also get to enjoy the benefits, now. So keep doing, keep thinking, and enjoy the benefits.

Memorable experiences

Ed Parker's home

Ed Parker lived at 1250 S. Los Robles in Pasadena. He asked me to come to the house for the first time when I was there in November 1979. I parked on the street out front and got out to look at the big, up-sloping lawn, the long driveway, and a sizable house bordered by hedges. I went up the front steps to the big double doors, rather amazed to find myself there. He answered and invited me in.

The Parker home was usually pretty busy. Often the extended family[25] was present, especially later in the 80s. They were doing administration for the IKKA, preparing for the Internationals, and the like. There would be grandchildren around, and his dogs were in the mix, too. A small "Benji"-type dog named Kawika (Kaa-vee-kaa, or David), Kapena (Captain), and later, by the time I came on the scene, Sushi, their black Labrador I used to scratch behind the ears.

---

[25] Sons-in-law Larry Kongaika and Nalu Tafua would be there, too, as would their children. Ed Parker's book company was called Delsby Publications, and the name came from the initials of the immediate family; Darlene, Edmund, Leilani, Sheri, Beth, and Yvonne.

We were heading to his office but I got the nickel tour first. In the hallway near his front door was a freestanding, square display case about four-and-a-half feet tall. The top foot was transparent and contained a pair of eyeglasses. The initials E.P. were in the bridge. Elvis Presley had given these glasses to Ed Parker. Etched on the display case was the quotation, "They have your initials on them, don't they?" with Elvis' name below.

A few feet farther down and partly into the hallway next to the stairs was a large, framed display box which hung on the left-hand wall with an engraved plate identifying the cape within as worn by Elvis at his *Aloha Hawaii* concert. Just a few steps past that you turned right down a hallway and found his office at the end on the left. On those hallway walls were many awards such as his *Black Belt Magazine* Man of the Year, other Hall of Fame induction awards, and the like. Not long after, a stained glass Universal Pattern we presented to him in Chicago would hang there also.

The office was not large. It had a window overlooking the pool and sliders facing the lanai. Bookshelves, file cabinets, magazine binders, his desk piled high with paperwork, a copy machine, and a chair or two jammed the room. You had to clear a place to sit. I remember numerous copies of his book, *Secrets of Chinese Karate,* which had been translated into other languages lining a high shelf, along with other filed items. More awards and certificates hung on the walls. This was where he was working on what would become the *Infinite Insights* books. He'd take calls here at Internationals time, answering questions about the tournament and telling the callers to "Bring your friends." This was where we'd sometimes talk, although the majority of my lesson time there was spent in the large living room. He was grinning as he showed me how he used economy of motion with his office copier, hitting the start button with his thumb as he closed the lid, pointing out how he needed minimal steps to do the job. When I looked at the items on the walls and remarked about how he had diplomas from many other organizations he dispensed this advice, "Be careful about what you accept. Once you take something from them, they can point at you as acknowledging their legitimacy." I consider that each time I am approached to accept an award or certificate.

One of my fondest memories of Ed Parker is of being at the house and we had gone back to sit in the TV room, next to the kitchen and opening onto the lanai. He put a tape in the VCR, telling me he wanted me to see it. One of the grandchildren sat down on the floor in front of the television and seemed to be entranced by the karate action onscreen. "He loves karate, can't get enough" he said, "He's gonna be my ass-kicker when he grows up." But what struck me was when his grandson Blake was brought in and he cradled him in his arms. He told me Blake had been a premature baby and was named after his friend, Blake Edwards. The contrast of the Ed Parker I knew, who manhandled black belts, and the doting grandfather who so gently held the baby is entrenched in my memory.

Ed Parker – (Tax) Fighter

I was with him one trip to Pasadena when he asked me to accompany him to order trophies for one of his tournaments. He selected the awards and was given a price. Casually leaning onto one elbow over the counter he told the owner he was a tax fighter and asked if the man would sell him the trophies at a "parts-only" price to beat the tax. They reached an agreement and the deal was sealed. If you hung out with Ed Parker long enough you found he was pretty generous with sharing knowledge but tight with the wallet.

Elvis, fan clubs, and the Elvis Cadillac

Mr. Parker described himself as a "protective companion" to Elvis, not a bodyguard. At times he traveled with Elvis on tour and would wear the tour jacket when he went to do seminars in various locations. He told stories of Elvis and would often draw Elvis fan club members to seminars and tournaments I held in Chicago. They'd come to watch the tournament and he'd speak with their group out in the lobby, signed autographs and posed for pictures with them.

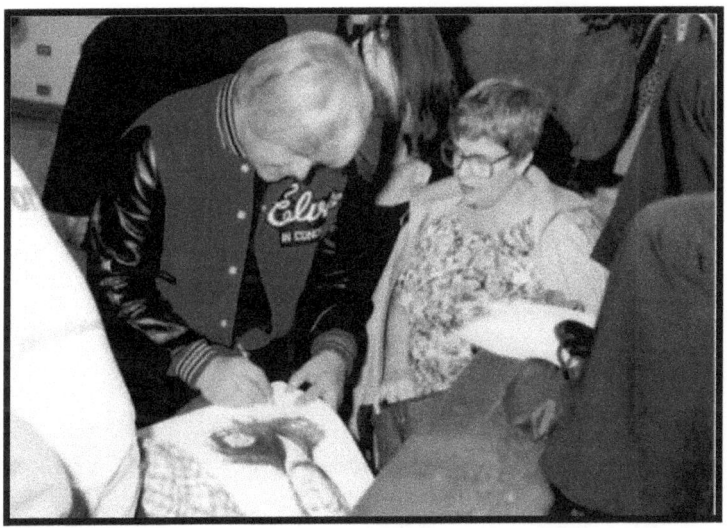

Ed Parker signs a portrait for my mother.

The president of the largest fan club in the Chicago area came to several seminars to rub elbows with Ed Parker and once took him out to his home to show him his collection of Elvis memorabilia. When he heard that EP was coming to my studio one time he called me and asked if he could host a dinner at a local restaurant at which Ed Parker would be the guest of honor. I contacted Mr. Parker and he told me he was ok with that. That day at the end of the seminar the man came to pick up Mr. Parker at my studio. The intent was for him to take him the few blocks down the street to the restaurant and I would come by later to get him back to his hotel. Parker pointed at me as he said to the man "I'm not going unless he goes." Imagine my surprise, standing there in a sweaty T-shirt and planning to go home to shower after the workout, not to dinner. We decided I would take Mr. Parker to the hotel to change and then to the restaurant, where we would meet the group. This we did, and when I got him to the hotel he said to me that I had to get him out of this. The club had about 80 people waiting for him and we couldn't blow them off so I concocted a strategy to make an early departure. We got to the restaurant and made our way back to the banquet room reserved for the dinner. As we walked through the restaurant, the fans saw us coming and started applauding, which got the attention of the diners in the restaurant proper. There was a lot of excitement, and they crowded around him. He didn't get much chance to eat since they were lined up for autographs and asking questions. After about an hour he gave me a prearranged signal and I walked out of the restaurant, returning a few minutes later. "Mr. Parker", I said rather loudly, "They're ready for us at the next stop." This tactical withdrawal kept everyone happy; the fans who certainly understood he was in demand, the club president, who had pulled off a bit of a coup by having him there, and Ed Parker, who was tired from traveling, teaching, and entertaining. They'd have kept him there for quite some time, and you can't blame them for that. He needed a break, but kept his word and showed up. That particular fan club was known in Chicago for raising lots of money for worthwhile charities and I like to think EP helped keep their flame burning, too.

Elvis had given him a Cadillac, like he did for so many others. It was a white, four-door Fleetwood Brougham. The story of how Elvis gave it to him and a photo of the car are in Ed Parker's book, *Inside Elvis*. He asked me to go with him to a meeting and we jumped in the car. As we motored along he said, "This is the car Elvis gave me", obviously proud of that. So that was cool, riding with Ed Parker in his Elvis-mobile. Mr. Parker also had a Chevy El Camino he drove a lot, and a Volkswagen GTI (like a Rabbit). It was funny to see that big guy get out of that little car. What wasn't funny was to see him get out of my Corvette by grabbing the top of the frameless window and hoisting himself up.

After I'd gotten to know Ed Parker he made a comment about Elvis that has stuck with me ever since. "Too bad you never got to meet him" he said, "He'd have liked you."

The International Karate Championships – 1977-1988

The IKC was always held in August. I went to my first in 1977 with my student, Kurt Barnhart, who was a purple belt at the time. He was eliminated in the first 30 seconds of his first match by punching someone in the head.[26] I lost my first round, too, when I fought Kenny Finister, who would eventually win the middleweight division and fight for Grand Champion. That was how my luck ran in some tournaments. I'd fight the eventual winner in the first round, but I gained some valuable experience in the process from fighting great fighters.

This event was COOL. There were thousands[27] of people there and lots of famous faces; Ed Parker, Steve Armstrong, Roy Kurban, Steve Fisher, Malia Dacascos,

---
[26] No headshots were allowed at all in the white to blue division.
[27] Up to 4,500 according to Tom Kelly, who was the tournament coordinator.

Mike Stone, Chuck Norris, Dan Anderson, Benny "The Jet" Urquidez, Tadashi Yamashita, Bill Wallace, Keith Vitali, and Bong Soo Han, to name a few I got to meet. And that's not to mention all the Kenpo people I also met.

That first year we went we were standing in the longest, slowest line for registration I'd ever seen. It took hours to get in the door. As we waited Ed Parker approached, heading in to get the show on the road. I pointed him out to Kurt and said, "There's Parker". The man in front of me turned around and said "Mr. Parker", emphasizing the Mister. I got it. Up until then I'd never seen him except on television once on the *Dinah Shore Show* when he thumped Larry Tatum. Anyway, we got our IKC patches to wear proudly on our *gis*, competed, lost, and went out to drink lots of beer with a friend on Redondo Beach. We had no idea what the Sunday night finals were like and missed them. It wasn't until a year or two later that we decided to go see the finals, which would usually run until midnight or 1am, by which time we were headed to the airport to catch the red-eye flight home to Chicago. The 1977 tournament was where I introduced myself to him for the first time, before all the action started. I gave him my card, got a picture with him, and got out of his way. He was friendly and didn't seem rushed but I knew with an event that size he was busy.

In following years we returned with more competitors. We'd head out on Thursday, go to Disneyland or Universal Studios on Friday, then attend the black belt meeting Friday evening and compete over the weekend. When I was asked by a student how much that IKC patch cost, because they didn't know what it was and thought they could buy one, I'd say $300. They'd be shocked and I'd explain the cost of airfare, room, food, entry fee, etc.

In 1979 I managed to place third in the men's medium forms division, out of 50 or 60 competitors, and earned the pagoda-style trophy the IKC was known for. I placed ahead of Frank Trejo, who I'd seen the previous years doing excellent forms and who would go on to compete for the forms Grand Championship at a later IKC. This particular year George Chung, a nationally-rated Tae Kwon Do practitioner, decided to run a form in our division. It wasn't a hard-style form but it wasn't a soft form either, so they let him in and he took second behind John Sarmousakis from Delaware, who ran a version of Tiger and the Crane. This put Frank in fourth place. As the division broke up, and Frank and I were standing together he collared Chung. "Don't you ever compete in this division again!" he exclaimed and punched him square in the chest. Chung never did compete in Kenpo forms at the IKC after that.

As years went by I'd see demos by Ed Parker with a variety of assistants such as Frank, Larry Tatum, Huk Planas, Jeff Speakman, Dian Tanaka, Bryan Hawkins, and more. I saw a man do a nunchaku demo with a live rattlesnake in his other hand. After he finished he had a plaque for Mr. Parker that he presented with the plaque in one and the snake in the other. Mr. Parker ambled up, accepted the plaque and returned to ringside without batting an eye. What was the man trying to accomplish? Your guess is as good as mine.

One year I fought "Smiley" Urquidez, Benny "The Jet"s brother. Both Benny and Blinky Rodriguez were ringside, both of them being world-class fighters, and adding support for the brother. It was one of those knock-down, drag-outs with the referee having to pull us apart. He launched a double step-through spin kick that I knew if I backed up he would hurt me, so I stepped in for the jam, started a kick to the crotch that turned into a knee and saw my boot come up by the side of his head. We went down, both still fighting and they broke it up. It was now overtime, tied score. He shot a back-knuckle that scored and it was over. Chuck Norris came over afterward and told me he had been watching and that he liked my hook kick.

The IKC was a long, long weekend. The tournament always started later than scheduled on Saturday morning and could run until the wee hours of Monday morning. The judges meeting on Friday went for hours. Ron Chapel ran it poolside at the Vagabond motel, near the Long Beach Sports Arena, where the tournament was held. One guy stood in a horse stance the whole time! At a later event, with the pool area jammed with people as it always was, I heard a commotion, looked in the general direction, and saw a chair fly through the air. Two bodies followed, locked together, and they went into the pool. It was Frank Trejo, who had a guy in a headlock and was trying to drown him as well as punch him. The story was that Frank had caught him trying to take something out of Ed Parker's room.

As I became more integrated into the Parker organization I would go out a day earlier than in the previous years. This allowed me to go to the class that Mr. Parker would run for out-of-town black belts at the Pasadena school on Thursday evening. In 1981 I was in a class with Rainer Schulte from Germany, Gary Ellis from England, and others from Spain and parts of the U.S. That was really my first contact with Gary. We'd meet again in Jersey about four years later and in 2003 he'd become my first seventh degree. I saw Mr. Parker knock out Frank Trejo in this class. Frank and I had been promoted, he to fourth and I to third, with Frank passing his belt down to me. We were feeling pretty good and we let our discipline drop a notch even though we were in the number one and number two positions in the class line. Mr. Parker was teaching *Leaping Crane* and its extension. He had Frank come up so he could work on his body. When he sent him back to his place in line Frank started to "moon-walk" there – and that's when the Old Man decided to continue his demonstration. He pulled him back as he was talking, did the base moves, and when he got to the extension changed the lifting back kick into a side kick and the back of his leg whacked Frank in the back of his skull. Frank was facing me and I saw his eyes roll up in his head, just before he pitched over on his face. It was one of those knockouts that the guy wakes up when they hit the floor. Frank jumped up and I think he bowed or saluted, then walked back to his spot. He whispered to me as he passed, "I was out". My reply was, "I know." You never saw two guys straighten their act up so fast.

    I met Kenpo black belt Jack Farr at the IKC. Jack was a "Triple Crown" competitor, according to one of the magazines, which meant he was top-rated in fighting, forms, and weapons. Jack and I became friends. We discussed techniques and he showed me an interesting variation on *Circling Wing* that I liked. When I got to my next private session with Mr. Parker I showed him what I had picked up. "You like that?" he said. "Do that on me."

Uh-oh. Next thing I know I had a thumb in my eye. "You have to use common sense in your checks," he said. He additionally gave me another example of why we did things a certain way to prevent such accidental or intentional moves. That simple question helped me realize so much about the structure of Kenpo techniques.

I'd met world-famous knife maker Gil Hibben at the IKC in 1981 or so and we've been friends ever since. Gil had trained alongside my teacher, Mike Sanders, and when we first met he commented on how much Mike and I looked alike, so much so we could have been brothers. The IKC is where I met Huk Planas and Tom Kelly for the first time, too.

One year I was invited by Mr. Parker to take a seat at ringside for the finals. That was a treat. What I remember most about it, though, was him losing his temper with someone or something and slamming his hand down on the table. It was scary. I can only imagine some of the things he had to deal with on an IKC weekend, based on what little I knew about the people involved and the mechanics of running such an event. He was entitled to lose it a bit.

I'm glad I made it to the Internationals. It was fun, I saw a lot of interesting and dynamic demos, (and some pretty crazy stuff), and met a lot of people. It was for us Kenpo people, it was huge, and it was an experience.

Five Swords

He did this technique so many times in so many places it deserves its own commentary. As I watched the seminar videos I saw him teach this technique to illustrate common principles such as alignment, power principles, contouring, flow, inserts, breathing, script or shorthand motion, and more. What is fascinating is how he did it differently at different times, and certainly in other venues around the world. I saw him do the version as it is in the Long Two form, starting with the inward block and a slicing chop. He did a variation with the block followed by a lifting chop, and yet another with a two hand block and lifting chop. Some versions were done with an inward block below the elbow and a rear hand check, others with a form of double block, using the front hand to strike the bicep. The two-hand version was done with the block/lifting chop in a shorthand manner, ricocheting off the block into the strike in one move.

Teaching the techniques and forms differently from place to place and across time created some confusion. Why did he do it? Maybe because the physical position of the attacker in the technique dictated it, possibly he was rethinking a technique, working it out for a change in the future. Did he forget that he taught it one way in one place and another somewhere else? He told me he intentionally did that in some places. Much of this can be set aside with the thought that all the versions he did worked, just as he told us that ten black belts could do it ten ways and still be right. A studio does need one standard way as a reference sequence to minimize confusion within the studio but variations should be known and taught as appropriate. I learned from the variations, and still do. That is what I think is the intended result.

Ohio seminars

Occasionally I would get a phone call from Mr. Parker asking if I would be able to meet him in Ohio when he would go there to teach. Being the Midwest representative for the IKKA he expected me to be there, and I always agreed to go since learning from him was always something to be taken when offered. Not to mention, he was enjoyable to hang out with.

I met him in Cleveland a few times at events hosted by different individuals, and once in Toledo. At one of the Cleveland seminars, a relocated California black belt who knew him came up to talk after the seminar. He was the type of guy who would tell you all about the technique and principles, even if you were Ed Parker. That apparently was irritating. When this instructor proceeded to elaborate on *Glancing Salute* (even though he was the one who asked a question) Mr. Parker simply said, "Show me" and did the prescribed attack. When the man stepped up to break the arm, he over-stepped, setting his foot past Mr. Parker's front foot. That would turn out to be bad. Mr. Parker turned away and back-scoop kicked him square in the groin – hard enough to lift him – as he walked away saying that was what would happen, how the man stepped past the line that allowed him to check, etc. Thing was, the guy was in street clothes and, judging from how big his eyes got, obviously wasn't wearing a cup.

At another seminar a black belt approached him afterwards to ask a question about the half- and quarter-beat timing he had mentioned in his seminar. The man had been asking question after question during the day, and I guess he was getting rather tired of him and seized an opportunity. He worked the man into a position off an attack and then hit him three times in the solar plexus with an outward heel-palm, shuffling in as he did – Wham! Wham, Wham! He hit him so hard in a short distance I could see his chest flex

through his *gi* and he was driven into the wall. As he bounced off the wall, I saw the big eyes and the master walked off saying once again, "And that's how it works...."
The next day that man stuck to me to ask questions instead of Mr. Parker.

I had brought some guys with me from Chicago to another event. It was a very small seminar, only six people; most were from my school. In later years when I had a small seminar somewhere I didn't feel bad. If it happened to him it could certainly happen to me. At this seminar, one of my brown belts, a young guy named Joe Merritt, happened to be the "dummy" for his demonstration of *Parting Wings*. When he got to the chop to the ribs, he liked to show the insert move in which you grab the pectoral muscle and squeeze. It has the delightful effect of getting the man on his toes. Joe got his money's worth. The next day he showed us the individual bruises made by each finger and the thumb. Apparently, Mr. Parker liked to do this because I've run into people around the world who have experienced the same bruising. There's something to be said for consistency.

Mr. Parker would often have one of his black belts around when he'd travel. It made some of his teaching easier because his people knew how to go with the techniques and could help out in large groups. Many seminars he did in the 80s were for people either switching or thinking about switching to the Parker system from other systems of Kenpo. Some became IKKA members and some didn't. There were what he called "fence-riders", learning the system or hosting seminars but not teaching what he was passing on. Many of those people were later asked to leave the association for that reason. A few would even wear patches from both groups on the same *gi*; something I knew bothered him. I learned a lot about Kenpo, Ed Parker, and the politics of the karate world by being able to attend such events with him.

Years later, after his passing, I read an article in *Black Belt* magazine in which an Ohio man claimed to have been not only Ed Parker's student but a close friend. In the eleven years I was the IKKA Midwest representative, and my area included Ohio, I don't ever remember hearing his name or meeting him, although meeting him was possible, for I met many people and I didn't remember names/faces. He was wearing a seventh degree in the photo in the article. I think I'd have known someone with a high rank in my region. Huk Planas said after Mr. Parker died, "He had more students after he died than when he was alive."

There was a promoter in Cleveland who had EP come in for a seminar and I was asked to be there, too. The man picked me up at the airport there and drove me to the venue. When I saw Mr. Parker I told him I thought there was something not quite right about the man. He anxiously wanted to know. I told him I couldn't put my finger on it and he asked me to let him know immediately if I figured it out. As it turned out, the event was not well attended, he bounced his check to Mr. Parker, and later skipped town when it was found that he had been molesting underage female students at his club. He never made good to Mr. Parker, and we couldn't find him. In a related story, a man shook hands with Mr. Parker, reintroducing himself. Mr. Parker remembered him. The man owed him money, having bounced a check, and Ed Parker not only remembered the amount owed but the color of the check!

I was to meet him there in Ohio once and our flights came in about the same time. There were enough men there to greet us that we needed to take two cars to our destination. He was in the first car and I was in the second. Someone in the first car must have asked a question about some technique because we saw him grab somebody and we could see the car was shaking as it was rolling along. That got quite a bit of laughs.

Wedding reception at the Parker home

I was invited to the reception for the double wedding of two of his children to be held at the house. Edmund Jr. and Jan, along with daughter Yvonne and Dan were married on December 10, 1982. The reception was a week later on the 18th. It was an honor to be there. I had known Ed Jr. because I was at the house regularly and we had become friendly. There's a picture on the Internet that was taken that evening of some of the Pasadena boys and Paul Girard is mistakenly identified as being me. There were a lot of people there, with many SoCal black belts in attendance.

I have Ed Parker's belt

A few years after his father passed away Ed Jr. was at one of the weekend camps we held in Ft. Myers, Florida. He told me he had something for me. With Steve White and Dr. Len Brassard present in the room said he thought his father's friends should have something of his and gave me one of his dad's *gi* jackets. It's one of the old "war" *gis*, a faded black cotton one. Most times you'd see him in his Tokaido, the one that didn't fade. They were a 50/50 cotton/poly bend that helped them hold their color and not wrinkle. It was a great *gi*. I had one when I was a green belt. It cost $25 back then.

I have his *gi* in a Plexiglas presentation case. It's now displayed at Steve White's Manchester Karate Studio in New Hampshire. There is a black belt tied around the waist. The belt is one of four passed down to me by Mr. Planas. Huk told Steve White that Ed Parker passed one of those belts to him, and Steve called me to ask if I knew which one was the Grandmaster's. Huk had never told me any of those belts were Mr. Parker's at one time, so I called him to ask which one was the Parker belt and he said he didn't remember. So, I have one of Ed Parker's belts but I don't know which one it is.

It's an honor to have a belt passed to you. Frank Trejo passed me his third and fourth degree black belts, Huk his fifth, sixth, seventh, and eighth degree belts. They are excellent practitioners. Once passed to you, it is incumbent that you uphold the rank by word and deed. Return of any belt can be asked for and it is especially embarrassing in the martial arts world to get such a request. This action is normally well thought-out before the request is made due to the weight of such a decision. It happens rarely.

Professor Chow's funeral

We had a very short conversation about his trip to Hawaii and attending his teacher's funeral. He was a bit distressed that he was the only one of the old group to be there but his main thrust was about how some did *kata* on the professor's grave. He seemed to like the idea, and in retrospect, I have to wonder if he was dropping a hint. I apparently was not the only person he told this to. The idea was bandied about at his funeral in Pasadena. I was told that Leilani did not like the idea at all and it was dropped.

When I went to the 1993 IKC, we rented a car and went to the Pasadena school where we ran into Larry Kongaika, one of the Parker sons-in-law. Larry was heading back to the house and allowed my guys to come along, which was a treat for them. Then we went to the Glendale cemetery where he is buried. My friends gave me a few minutes alone at the grave. I used that time to press my hand down onto the IKKA crest that is raised on the metal marker there, making its impression on my hand, as I thanked him again for all he had done. I'd have felt strange doing *kata* on his grave as a sign of respect but I do show that respect for him each and every time I do a form.

Other events, stories, and analogies

The Port-a-gee

"Port-a-gee" is taken from Melville's *Moby Dick* and refers to one of Portuguese extraction. Ed Parker was rather proud of the fact that he was of that heritage. Portuguese sailors traveled the globe and many landed and stayed in Hawaii. Parker's mother must have transmitted that pride to him; she even had a Portuguese flag in the house.

I was with him on some of his East Coast trips when the guys from New Bedford, Massachusetts, Leo Lacerte and his student Lance Soares, would bring him linguica, a spicy Portuguese smoked sausage. He really enjoyed the stuff and Leilani would comment on that fact when she met Lance many years later, telling him about how much he loved it and appreciated their gift. His eyes would light up when they would give it to him, Leo often sliding it out from the inside of his coat as if it were contraband, which would always get a laugh. Lance related years later that Leilani told him it would make his gout flare up something fierce.

The Organ Grinder

When Ed Parker was at King Kamehameha high school he had a teacher who told him he would never amount to anything. Many seminar groups heard this story and that when he grew up he returned to look for that teacher, implying he might wreak havoc on him. "What do you think I did when I found him?" he said, rather darkly. "I shook his hand and thanked him." It turned out that the teacher's statement served to motivate him endlessly. He often continued with an analogy to the monkey and the organ grinder, describing a pairing that was common in the early 20th century where a man would play a portable organ and had trained his monkey to dance. Passersby would put money in a cup, providing an income for them both. Ed Parker would say "I'd rather be the organ grinder than the monkey", attributing much of his motivation to be successful to those words from his former teacher.

Sam Ting

When Ed Parker would teach he would sometimes show one move, then another similar or related move, and say "Sam Ting". But why the "Sam Ting"? His story went that there was a Chinese man named Tim O'Reilly. How did he get what was obviously an Irish name? He was in line at immigration, waiting to be admitted to the United States. The man in front of him was Irishman who told the official his name was Tim O'Reilly. The Chinese man said that when he came up next and was asked his name he told the official his name was Sam Ting, so they wrote his papers up as Tim O'Reilly. "Same thing, Sam Ting", Parker would laugh as he shrugged his shoulders. And he always told the story with the "R" pronounced as an "L" – Tim O'Leilly. He attributed the story to Bruce Lee.

The slow-motion cigarette

In the April 1981 seminar he defined *chi* as the instant harmonizing of the conscious and subconscious mind. He believed that combination was what allowed chemicals in the body to be released that would "Bring out the genie inside." He then told his famous story about driving with Leilani when four men pulled them over back in 1956. "Nine times I've used my Kenpo and three times it saved my life", he said. "This was the first time that everything was in slow motion. Twice before it was, like, in and out; fast, then slow. This time it was all slow." He continued by describing how two men closed in on him with two more waiting, apparently thinking it would only take two to do the job on him. "The first guy threw a right, and I was thinking about how I could hit his ribs, but that wasn't what I wanted. Then I saw he was wearing a white shirt and I realized I could have a psychological advantage if I could hit him and make him turn so that his friend would see the blood on the shirt." He did just that, and the friend hesitated just long enough that Parker hit him in the head, too, hard enough to make his cigarette go flying upward, which he saw turning end-over-end in slow motion. "The other two guys went and locked themselves in the car", he said as he laughed. "Now, I've dropped about 26 guys in my life and they all dropped like rag dolls. This guy (with the cigarette) went stiff like a board and his head hit the ground. That scared me. I did not want to take his life. After a few minutes, his legs moved and I knew he was alive."

Years later I had the opportunity to ask Leilani about that incident. She had been pregnant with their first child and didn't want him to pull over but "Ed liked to fight". She put her hands to her face and said, "He was an animal!" She confirmed he thought he had killed the second guy and was naturally very relieved to see he was moving.

The Kapu

There was a Chicago man named Tom Letuli whose son, Freddie, was a tournament competitor. Both have passed away. One year Freddie went to the Internationals and placed fourth in one of the divisions.[28] It was not uncommon that when that happened a fourth place plaque was not available and you were told it would be sent to you.

Freddie and his father waited for a few months and no plaque was forthcoming. Tom, the son of Samoan royalty, gave me a message to give to Mr. Parker the next time I saw him. It was, "Tell him if I don't get that plaque I'm going to put the *kapu* on him!" Being a white boy from Chicago I had no idea what it meant and when I had asked Tom he said, "Just tell him!" On my next trip to Pasadena, I gave Mr. Parker the message and asked what it meant. He said, "It's the Kahuna curse." So there I was, just having told the master of our system that someone was going to put some Polynesian curse on him for not getting his trophy. Freddie Letuli got his plaque; I delivered it. Both Tom and Ed Parker have passed away, and I'm sure it was not from a curse.

---

[28] The IKC flyer often advertised 1st through 4th place awards, with trophies for 1st, 2nd, and 3rd, and a plaque for 4th. Sometimes there just were not enough to go around.

Death premonitions

At the April 1981 Chicago seminar Mr. Parker stated that he believed in the power of the Hawaiian Kahunas, telling the group he saw one Kahuna do something to his father that caused him to go blind in one eye. His dad went to another Kahuna who restored him. He followed with a story about that particular Kahuna making his own funeral arrangements. As he told it, the man went into a funeral parlor and asked for a particular size and shape of coffin. When asked who it was for man the told the funeral director it was for himself. Naturally the funeral director had a bit of difficulty believing it, especially as the man specified the day and time of his passing. The Kahuna wanted it to be ready for Friday of the following week at 8:00 and said he would be there at 7:45. The days went by and on the designated day and time he arrived, at 7:59 he laid down in the coffin, and at 8:00 he was pronounced dead. Ed Parker said, "I believe this", and he attributed it to the Kahuna's ability to synchronize his conscious with his subconscious.

Now why did Ed Parker tell a story like that? I think there were two reasons. First, he used such stories to show how the conscious and unconscious mind worked together to make things appear to happen in slow motion, to generate tremendous power, and for things like this. Second I believe it was based on his premonitions. Joe Palanzo told me how he and Ed Parker were together in 1978 or 1979 when Mr. Parker got a very strange look on his face. Joe asked him what was wrong and the reply was that he had a very strong feeling he was going to die. Coincidentally one of Mr. Parker's brothers died in Hawaii that next day. That feeling is what motivated him to re-energize his teaching of the system, not wanting it to be lost if he should pass prematurely. It was about that time that he took me on as a private student, as well as some others in the subsequent year or so. He went into writing full-bore, with the *Infinite Insights into Kenpo* series being part of the result.

Ed Parker, Jr. told me that his dad started to organize his writings, notes, files, etc. not long before he died. Ed said to me, "He knew he was going to die." I believe this based on the stories Mr. Parker told, the stories I was told about him, and my personal experiences with him. But if this was an emergent pattern I think he <u>did</u> know he was going to die and he was taking the appropriate steps. But why he didn't "appoint a successor" as one of those steps is the subject of much speculation.

I had been told that the Kahuna he mentions in the first part of the story was his father. Upon checking with Edmund Jr. he said he had not heard that but did say his grandfather had predicted his own death and told me his grandfather said he would die on his feet and that is what happened.

The story of Sam Brown

Mr. Parker would often end a seminar with the story of Sam Brown and Abraham Lincoln.

"Sam Brown was an enemy of Abraham Lincoln. One day they collided with each other and Sam Brown challenged Lincoln to a duel. What do we know about Sam Brown? That he was small in stature and that Lincoln was well over 6' 4". Brown was also an expert with an axe. Lincoln said, "You have challenged me, yet I get to select the time, the weapon, and the place. When? Tomorrow morning at dawn, with an axe. Place? In the river, under six feet of water." Parker continued, *"How tall was Sam Brown?"* He related that Brown then congratulated Lincoln as the first man to beat him verbally and they became friends. *"So, when you are challenged, you say the time is now and the place is a phone booth. Invite him in and close the door."*

Since the time he told this story to illustrate the value of using your wits instead of your hands and that you can nullify an opponent's kicking advantage by getting "phone booth" close, phone booths are largely gone.

Are we losing the gist of the story for future students? Had he lived I am sure he would have found another captivating way to get his point across. I have a student, Bruce Meyer, who wrote the preface to the first edition of this book and Bruce has an actual phone booth in his back yard. This photo was taken in a Florida museum.

Knowing where to hit

This story is popular in management circles and appears frequently. For us, it emphasizes how important it is to know where to hit. I teach my students that the root of any art of self-defense is in knowing how, when, and where to hit. It was taught early on in the Parker system as Timing, Tools, and Targets.

A factory owner's large, expensive machine broke down and he called in an expert to fix it. When the man arrived he looked over the machine for a minute, took out a hammer and tapped one particular spot. The machine started immediately and ran normally. The owner was ecstatic. The expert then gave him a bill for $2,000. The owner complained that the expert had only been there for a few minutes, the charge was exorbitant, and would not pay. The expert took him to court.

The factory owner told his side of the story to the judge. When the judge asked the expert what he had to say in his defense he told the judge that $50 was for the time spent on the call and the other $1950 was for having the expertise of knowing where to hit. The case was decided in favor of the expert.

Handyman Sam

Another closing story was of a man who bought a gizmo and took it home. After being unable to assemble it using the instructions he looked out the window and saw his handyman, Sam, outside. He called Sam inside and asked him to put it together. In just a few minutes, without even looking at the instructions, he had it together. "How did you do that?" the employer asked. "Boss, I can't read. And when you can't read you gotta think." Ed Parker said we don't really take time to think about what we do. He stressed over and over how simple the things are that we do and how they relate to so many things we have and experience in our lives. Kenpo is sophisticated simplicity.

Cheap Shirts

Ed Parker told seminar participants that he observed new students who, when grabbed by the lapel, would focus on the attack and try counter-grabbing the arm with both hands and attempt to peel it off. In the process they ignored the fact that while they tried that the opponent would punch them in the face. "Cost of shirt, $5. Cost of face, $25." For historical context, I add that you'd want to know he said the shirt was bought at Sears, the cost being in dollars at that time and that the cost to fix your face today is significantly higher. As he physically demonstrated with both hands on the attacker's wrist and failing to twist, he'd take the partner's other arm and work it like a punch to his face. Then he'd demonstrate a basic technique striking the arm, his point was that you should not waste time and should be aware of their follow-up potential. "Trust your art".

Law Enforcement stories

At the 1982 nunchaku seminar in Chicago he knew there were several police officers in the crowd. They had asked questions so he diverged from the subject toward the end of the seminar to address some of these subjects. He told of how he had gotten a man into a jail cell when local officers had been working on him for 30 minutes and couldn't. The suspect was holding onto the cell door bars and bracing himself with his feet as the officers were hitting his limbs with their clubs, to no effect. Ed Parker was there at the station because of his relationship with the police and they asked him if he could do anything. He looked at the situation and immediately saw what needed to happen. He buckled one leg as he fulcrumed the suspect's chin and twisted, which shot the man into the cell so hard he bounced off the back wall, and Mr. Parker closed the door. You can imagine how wide-eyed the officers were. It was funny to see how he set up the demonstration of how he did it at the seminar and played the role of the suspect to see if anyone had a solution to the problem. He had a huge grin on his face when one man said he thought he knew what to do, that being to grab and spin him, so he said, "Grab me". The group laughed and when he was grabbed he immediately countered it with flow and power.

He told another story about being detained at the Mexican border with another black belt. While there he spoke to the other man and the officer told him to shut up. He said there were no signs saying he had to be quiet and they should have one in English and Spanish if this were so. This of course irritated the officer who told him to get up against the wall and spread his legs. "That's what I was waiting for", he said with some glee. The officer started to search him and Mr. Parker buckled his leg to take him down. He says the officer asked him how he did that and now he became the teacher instead of the detainee. He showed us the best position to search someone that eliminated the leverage points he had used by assuming the position the officer had asked for. If he had done that in today's world he likely have been shot, Maced, or Tasered and would be doing some jail time. I don't know when this occurred but there was a time when police tactics were not as advanced as they are today. What he showed us is very much like the advanced material I learned as a police defensive tactics instructor in the late 1970s. Whether he invented the tactics and passed them on or it was a matter of simultaneous development is open to question. The fact remains his approach was sound. Whether this actually happened, I don't know, but it illustrated his point.

In a third story he said he disarmed a police officer, taking his pistol and holding it to his head. I'd heard the story two different ways but with the same technique shown. In both versions he canceled the officer's lead side, spun his back to him in a rolling body check while maintaining the check on the officers lead side, snatched the gun out of the officer's holster, and held it to his head. Again, in today's world this would be almost impossible because of better training on the part of the officers and the development of weapon-retaining holsters and physical techniques. Back in the 1950s and 1960s it certainly could have been done. I tend to doubt the part about holding the gun to the officer's head because I don't think he'd take the chance on accidentally shooting the officer. But I could be wrong.

Mr. Parker liked to take credit for getting officers doing traffic stops to position their cars on an angle behind the vehicle they pulled over. Back then it was procedure to pull behind in line with the offender so he said he asked why they did not park on an angle so the engine block could be used as an obstruction, not just a car door, should gunfire occur. Today we see that applied in almost every stop. Was it his idea? Maybe.

Other memories

Hanging out with Ed Parker was a life-changing experience. I got to see him as a teacher, but also as one of the guys. I remember him telling me that sometimes he'd like to go back to Honolulu and be a wharf rat; not the leader of the Kenpo world, but just one of the guys working the docks. Many of us feel like that from time to time and never act on it. It's a relief valve from the pressure of being a leader.

We went to Garden Grove for a meeting he had to attend. I waited out by the car but on arrival he introduced me as one of his associates. Another man joined us and Ed Parker was introduced to him as "Ed Parker, Master of Kenpo Karate". While sitting in the car I happened to look in the mirror and saw him standing on the sidewalk. His associate approached him from behind and started to apply a forearm choke in a gentle, teasing manner as he said something to Ed. I saw his hand go up automatically to grab-check the arm, but in a correspondingly relaxed manner as they laughed and his friend let go. He was "one of the guys".

After a class at Pasadena a group of us went to a local Mexican restaurant for lunch. Frank Trejo and Mr. Parker were the only ones I really knew and neither of them very well. This may have been the first week I was at Pasadena to train. I remember sitting at the table across from Mr. Parker and he was staring at me. At first I thought he was looking out the window behind me and I actually turned around to see what he was looking at. There wasn't anything of interest and I saw that he really was staring at me. It was uncomfortable to say the least. A year later I told that story to Joe Palanzo who said, "The Old Man was trying to intimidate you." Well, it worked. As I told the story to others I found that he did that somewhat often. I'm glad he thought it was funny.

We were in a Chinese restaurant in the evening after one of the seminars in Chicago, May 1983. This place had a Hawaiian revue, with a Hawaiian entertainer and hula girls. Perfect! About 20 of us were there, including my parents. While we ate and watched the show a funny thing happened. The entertainer was playing his guitar and singing and looking over the crowd, then squinting hard as he saw Ed Parker. After his set he came to the table and asked him if he was, indeed, Ed Parker. The Old Man got a huge kick out of that and acknowledged that he was, which pleased the man. When he started his next set he announced his presence and even gave him the hand over fist salute. Such was the reputation of Ed Parker,[29] and amazing that he'd be recognized in a Chinese restaurant in the south suburbs of Chicago by another island boy, so far from home. Mr. Parker invited them to stop by the seminar the next day. They did, and brought the hula girls. Chairs appeared out of nowhere for them, you know how men are.

---

[29] He told me of driving down the freeway once and passed a group of Hell's Angels. One happened to look over, did a double take, and saluted.

Going out to eat with EP was fun and your own meal was fair game. "You gonna eat that?' became something of an "in-joke" with people who knew him. You wanted to make sure you didn't get your fingers near his mouth. Tom Kelly managed to get by him one day with an underhand chopstick pick to get his last piece of food right out of his hands. Bravo, *Si-bok!*

When he came to Chicago and was in the midst of working on the *Infinite Insights* series I arranged to get some portrait photos shot by a high school friend of mine named Brad Crooks. It is Brad's photos that appear when you see the black background headshots from time to time, as on the next page. They're all over the place today

Brad also shot the move-by-move photos that were used to draw the figures in Volume Five of *Infinite Insights* of me doing the forms. We shot everything from Short One through Long Three. Ed Junior found those photos in a box many years later. Ed did the drawings, giving me some more hair in the process, and altering the positions somewhat. He made line drawings of the salutation from the photos that were used not only in the book but also on t-shirts. It was strange seeing myself on those. It was a real honor to be the model for the books. In addition Brad shot most of the photos for my magazine articles over the years.³⁰

Photo by Brad Crooks

When the system manuals were rewritten in 1981, Ed Parker had me meet him at his Ed Parker Enterprises office in neighboring Glendora when I was in for one of my visits. I spent hours in that office making the first copies of the

---

³⁰ Coincidentally, Brad lives in **Parker**, Colorado now.

second-generation technique manuals that were done primarily by Jim Mitchell.[31] While I was in the office Mr. Parker called up and told me to lock the door, as there was a gunman loose in the building! (Nothing came of it.) The Mitchell manuals caused a shift in the system, some of which, in my opinion, was not for the better. I ran down to the Pasadena school with the first copies since Mr. Parker let me keep the first ones off the copier and got together with Frank Trejo. We had Paul Girard read aloud the write-up for the extension to *Twirling Hammers* as we worked it on each other. It wasn't working, and I remember Frank throwing the manual on the floor and stomping off to his office. Later, when I was in New Hampshire at Steve White's school with Mr. Parker, I asked him if he wanted us to learn the "new" material and he simply said, "Don't bother". I did pick up the new extensions, the "new" techniques, sets, etc but I don't normally teach them for many reasons. The real question is; why did we get this new curriculum and if he didn't think we needed to learn it, why

---

[31] I saw Jim many times over the years. One time I saw him sitting poolside at the Vagabond motel for one of the IKCs and Sandy Sandoval roundhouse kicked him in the head, hard. Mitchell was later thrown out of the IKKA for "deceitful" actions. I have the document, sent in 1983 by Ed Parker, to all IKKA schools.

have it? I can think of reasons but I don't really know why he did that.

One trip to Chicago he told me that the next time he saw me he was going to promote me. "Bump you up" was the phrase he used. When I made arrangements for my next trip out for training one of my black belts reminded me that I was going to be promoted and congratulated me. I told him he was premature but that's just my personality. Wouldn't you know that when I got to Pasadena, Mr. Parker was out of town for the week? Disappointing? Yes. Deterring? No. The stripe on the belt was not what I was after; it was knowledge and ability.

Jim Lowell and I were in goofing off California. I had told Mr. Parker I would be in SoCal and he told me to come by the house on a certain evening. I think he forgot to write it down because when we arrived the family was in the midst of starting dinner. They made space for us at the table, and were gracious hosts. Afterward he pulled out his ukulele and played Beatle songs. There were many times I was invited to eat at the Parker home and Leilani was always so friendly to me. From what he had told me that wasn't always the case and there were people she wouldn't allow in the house. Jim would later be in California and stop by the Pasadena studio when they asked him to be there for a photo shoot for one of the *Infinite Insights* volumes, so you'll see him in Volume Four.

I was sitting in the stands at the Internationals one year when he came and sat down with me. I asked him if he was taking a break and he told me he liked to see the event from the perspective of the spectator. In his teaching he told us to consider the third person perspective and here he was, practicing what he preached. As we watched, a competitor was onstage doing a weapons form and every time she kicked he recoiled, saying "I hate that". I asked what he meant and he pointed out that she tucked her head forward every time she kicked. "It cuts your reach", he told me. It's true. You can't kick as high with a front kick when you drop your head down and forward. Good lesson.

He once said to me that he could tell when I liked something he said or did "Because your eyes get big". I had been told that in my early days as an instructor I was serious and didn't smile much. One school owner even told me her goal was to get me to smile. I was starting to loosen up by the late 70s, especially being around Frank Trejo. Laughing in class was frowned on by some instructors and Joe Palanzo was the opposite. He laughed, the class laughed and everyone relaxed. It's been shown that enhances the learning experience and retention. Mr. Parker often said at the start of a seminar, "C'mon in, we're going to have a good time". I'm not the same person I was in the 70s and I've learned that getting an audience to laugh means they were paying attention.

I was with Mr. Parker one night at dinner when he got a strange look on his face. I asked him what was wrong and he said he realized that he had less time to live than he had already lived. I experienced that same thought after I crossed the 50-year mark myself. Now I understand.

"I was faster than Ed Parker."

His son and I were talking one day about his growing up with Ed Parker for a father and told me a funny story. As children will do, sometimes they get under a parent's skin. He riled up Dad one day and hid under a table to escape his wrath. When Dad made a grab for him, he evaded him, which led to his statement; "I was faster than Ed Parker."

Speaking with his daughter Darlene, she once told me he'd call down the hall from his office using each child's name until he got a response from the one closest. Good stuff.

The Audio Tapes

While most of this book's material was derived from my notes and seminar videos, I had seven one-hour audio cassettes I had been keeping for years. Most of them were from the first lessons in 1979, and others in 1980 and 1981. Two were of a seminar in Chicago. In 2023 I bought a converter so I could digitize them. Cassette players had been hard to find for some time but now they were coming back and incorporated the new technology. I found the tapes were still playable after over 40 years , if not of the best sound quality. And back then I was a young instructor in my 30s, and had not had the best training prior to getting to study with SGM Parker. I could hear a lot of hesitation in my voice. Many of the questions I asked are considered basic today but I just didn't have the depth of instruction. However, he was patient and took time to explain his concepts and principles to me. He saw something in me I didn't see in myself, and I am grateful.

I wrote earlier in the book what was on the tapes and here I extract much of that for you. There is some repetition but also lots of additional material.

Private Lesson

February 12, 1980

In this lesson he told me "You're asking me things nobody ever asked me before."

When discussing cover-outs (or whichever term you prefer) he stressed that the hands should coordinate with the legs and body to stabilize and counter-balance the action. He states there is a difference between a switch, cover and cover-out. I had also mentioned I had learned two cat stances, a close cat and extended cat. He was quick to correct me, no such thing.

We talked technicalities in which he told me to follow the circle of the ribs when punching, staying on center for proper alignment and back-up mass, to not put the brakes on a move prematurely. "Let the face of the target make the stop."

He clarified such things as a snap being the end result of a whip, that there are solid and ricochet elbow sandwiches and that the way I had been taught on sandwiches was "BS".

We discussed the salutation. He defined the moves, something he did not do in the *Infinite Insights* books. The moves are demonstrated but no meaning to each move is written. He showed me some of the self-defense applications in it. I told him that I had shown a form to my kung-fu teacher and he did not like our salutation, saying it said we were proud. Mr. Parker dismissed that.

There are two very interesting comments on the tape. In one I said I had read his manuscript. I believe this was when he sent me off with the draft to Volume 3. I stayed up all night reading. When I brought it back he asked if I "had any comments or corrections". Corrections? I didn't know enough to correct his work. But it did start a discussion about body maneuvers that he was excited about and that information was then included in the book. The other comment he made was that he was planning to get everything on video. A few years later when I asked him about that, he was opposed to it. It would be Larry Tatum who filmed and released it through Panther Productions after he was let go from the Parker business and organization.

I got him to talk about Professor Chow. He adamantly stated Chow studied with Mitose but "was not a direct descendant of Mitose" and "did not get all of his knowledge from Mitose." Chow learned from his father. I remember him saying at another time it was like a crane system. He also spoke of Mitose calling the system Karate Kenpo, that is was spelled with an "n" and that "Kenpo is as your last name is to your first".

We talked about training methods and students. What to do with those who were physically slow? How about someone not particularly motivated? And he recommended a drill to improve punching that had one person hold a staff in each hand and the puncher had to punch between them without hitting either. "They'll nip their knuckles" he said. He told me his operating principle in teaching was to review the material at least three times, emphasizing a second and third principle on the second and third reviews to drive the lessons home. I told him my previous training was short on principle and terminology, and he agreed.

I asked him about the lines in the IKKA patch, knowing they are indicative of the 18 Hands of Lo-Han. I told him we only figured out 16 directions and he replied I was "forgetting about the lines you can't see", those being forward an back.

In the last few minutes of the tape I hear him running me through orange belt techniques. He was looking to see if I used terms, understood principles and execute correctly.

We did *Locking Horns* (obscure zone), *Lone Kimono* (angle of cancellation), *Glancing Salute* (fulcruming), *Five Swords* (complementary angle), *Scraping Hoof* (compounding), *Grip of Death* (body fulcrum) and *Crossing Talon* (two types of grab). *Five Swords* was done with an inward block and a check, not the double block version we see so much today.

What I thought on listening again was that I seem to be much more comfortable with him and the conversation flowed better.

Private Lessons

February 13 and 14, 1980

We picked up where we left off the previous day and he covered the rest of the range belt techniques. He was doing what he said he would; reviewing to ensure more principles were understood and applied. It was good to hear him say "Very good, it's coming" and "beautiful". He made few corrections but did admonish me once or twice, saying "You're doing something I don't like." The two comments he made were key and something I see a lot of when I teach, even today. I was bobbing frequently and this correction reinforced how to stay grounded. The other point was to keep my elbows in and follow body contours when shifting to a reverse bow with a hammerfist. I can imagine that looking at orange material might have been boring for him. He'd taught me the techniques at the studio months before but these lessons were done in his home.

- *Shielding Hammer* – emphasis on the function of the dipping outward elbow

- *Thrusting Salute* – emphasis on the circle and square
- *Striking Serpent's Head*- emphasis on the brace and fulcrum with the left arm
- *Locked Wing, Obscure Wing, Reversing Mace, Buckling Branch, Thrusting Prongs* – no pointers or corrections
- *Twisted Twig* – he pointed out that the left checking hand could be used as a punch or poke as a prefix
- *Obscure Sword* – emphasis on the angle of the first step (straight ahead) and use of borrowed force
- *Repeating Mace, Raining Claw, Captured Leaves, Evading the Storm, Twirling Wings, Captured Leaves, Leaping Crane, Crushing Hammer, Circling Wing* and *Calming the Storm* all had no significant comments or corrections.

We covered a few purple belt techniques, *Thundering Hammer*, in particular. He did not pronounce the "s" on hammer. I recall this being the lesson he told me to learn the techniques from Frank Trejo, then show him what Frank taught me. "That way I can check both of you."

Belt colors were a topic. I asked about them because it seemed our purple and green belts were in reverse order to most systems I had encountered. He looked at the colors as if mixing paint and told me green was darker than purple. I don't see it but it's his system. Today, many studios have colors we did not use and it's a bit confusing. But it works for them.

The rest of the recording was in the car and was when I brought up the manuals. As I wrote earlier, he said the manual was written for beginners, to "provide them point of reference which is most safe". He reiterated that advanced students may alter techniques and that was fine.

I asked about Master Key moves. He defined it as a sequence that works for four or five different situations. His thinking was that a lot of students think they have to use a different sequence for each attack. Therefore, the Master Key was a tool to get them to understand that just is not always so.

I asked about checking and he told me that some techniques have a variable because "I want you to see the variables. You don't have to practice all the variables", but you should know of them.

Private Lesson

June 18, 1980

On this you can hear him very well but not me. That's due to keeping the recorder close to him to capture his answers but some of my questions are hard to hear. There's a lot of dead air, and I'm sure a better editor could tighten it up. One thing you can hear is a cough he had. I seem to remember him dealing with that a lot.

In the hour we talked about some pretty basic material. We discussed;

- Zone theory
- Definitions of punches and strikes
- Foot and body maneuvers
- Methods of execution
- Reacting vs countering
- Spinning vs twirling (spin has ground contact, twirl is airborne)
- Simultaneous action and points of origin to start
- Techniques

He said he chose the standing naturally position for most because it's awkward.

I asked him about what he thought the fastest natural weapon was and without hesitation he said it was a knife-edge kick to the shin. The shin basically has no defenses, he said. "He's jabbing at you, so you use your leg to keep him away."

During this lesson, we were interrupted an I hear myself reading some of quotes and definitions. Obviously, that was to remind myself but I mention it because I think this was what he was working on in preparing Volume 1 of *Infinite Insights into Kenpo*. This makes me think this lesson was June 1980, about two years before publication.

I'm telling you that because he told me, in that lesson, that "This is all good stuff. You're asking good questions." It was part of his methodology to talk with his black belts, hear and respond to their questions and incorporate such information into the books. He also told me that the plan was to have eight volumes.

I asked about when the techniques got names and his answer was 1960 or 1961. Some had names prior but he felt that naming sequences aided understanding, retention and motivation. "If I say next time we'll do another variation on this right punch defense, the effect is different than if I say next time we'll do Dance of Death."

It was that thinking that led to instituting colored belts. He thought color change versus just a new tab on the belt, which is what was done at first, there was motivation and a sense of status. He did not have a degree in psychology for nothing.

The lesson ended with us talking about business practices, such as putting students on contracts, protecting yourself from liability and having a corporation to help do so.

Seminar 1980

I have two cryptically marked cassettes from 1980.

He started with something he often said, which was he was there to share with the group, not to simply show. He wanted you to make that lesson yours and just showing you something was not going to do.

"Sounding out the moves", his analogy of motion to speech started it off. "We want you to understand the phonetics of motion to get the most power from an ideal position." He then touched on "letters of motion", "words of motion" ("Some of you guys would come up with a thesis") and then about using numeric values. He would expand on this, saying it was best to learn four moves and how to rearrange them than many moves without that understanding. His explosiveness can be heard on the tape. He ran the group through the formula of the Four Factorial using numbers and told a story of some "foreign individuals" at a demonstration he did who criticized his use of the elbow sandwich. "I called him up", and he continued by saying his famous line of "To hear is to doubt, to see is to be deceived but to feel is to believe." He worked the combination of the four moves he just did with the seminar group, asking them if a person would react a certain way to a strike and telling them the man did just that and ran into the elbow sandwich. He said the heel-palm allowed him to "get his money's worth". At other times I'd hear him say "You gotta brace the face so the face don't fly off into space." The man asked him to do it again, anticipating the same sequence and probably thinking he could thwart it. He tried, Mr. Parker changed it, nailed him, to the man's surprise and said "Like lightning, never hit twice in the same place." He smiled as he did a cover out to the laughter of the group.

When he got to the Eight Considerations, he told the group to prioritize the components, asking which was most important starting with saying range, then position, then environment. I think this was a brilliant way to get them to see his logic in ordering them. If you're familiar with them, you know environment was first. I say <u>was</u> because he'd later add Acceptance and make it first. He asks why "we read books that tell us what to do when it's happening? We should be reading about how to prevent it from happening".

Listening to the tapes reminds me of what a great presenter he was. He involved the class, got them laughing with his stories and analogies, made eye contact so people felt he was talking to them, altered the volume of his voice for emphasis when needed. He asks what the attitude is on the streets today. "It's not who's right, but who's left that counts." Such statements got people thinking.

He spoke and demonstrated for about 35 minutes before the group started working on each other. He understood, as I would later, that listening was only part of the reason people attended. Another part was to see him move. Over years of watching a variety of world-class instructors I realized what I call the "freak show" was a big part of the attraction. People want to see the speed and accuracy and get a sense of the power by watching or being worked on. It cemented lessons, or at least made the event memorable.

"There's no sense in learning any form if you don't know the meaning is. It's like learning a language while never learning it's definition." He went on to talk about one word having multiple definitions just as one move could as well. "Just as you have command of vocabulary, I want you to have command of motion."

In the last 15 minutes he talked about base moves. "They can be anything you want." He then said you can prefix, suffix, add, alter, delete, rearrange, insert and regulate.

He continued about not letting your ego be in control. "Make sure your head grows in proportion to your body." This was illustrated in Volume 1 of *Infinite Insights* with a cartoon. He ended with a story about a lion walking in the jungle. He sees a monkey and asks him "who is King of the Jungle?" The monkey says "You are" and the lion goes on his way. He sees a snake and asks the same question, getting the same answer. He sees and elephant and asks him too. The elephant picks him up with his trunk and slams him against a tree. The lion gets himself up and asks again, saying "I don't think you understood me." The elephant picks him up again, slamming him to the ground. The lion gets up saying, "Just because you don't know the answer you don't have to get mean." Mr. Parker said "If you get to that point where you are as dumb as that lion, it's time to get out of the martial arts."

A story about being on TV with Regis Philbin was last. Philbin asked is he was afraid of a gun. He told him he was not, it was the bullet in the gun he was afraid of.

Private Lesson

November 1980

It was now a year since I'd become a direct student of Ed Parker's. I brought Skip Hancock with me to this lesson. Skip had just come down from Spokane for the first time. He was hanging out at the Pasadena school and sleeping on the mat. Trejo had me run through the yellow material with him. I told Mr. Parker he was there and he asked me to decide whether to bring him up to the house, which I did. I like to think I was Skip's entree to Mr. Parker.

During this lesson I told Mr. Parker about how I see technique patterns like string art, the kind with colored string wrapped on nails and connected. He said he saw it like that too. It would be many years later that Bruce Meyer told a story about the first time he heard my name. He'd known who I was but it was at a seminar with Joe Palanzo that he heard Joe say about me, "He sees things in multiple planes simultaneously."

In this tape he says he had all the thesis form requirements for the various ranks all written out and would publish them. Ultimately, he didn't.

He bashed *Black Belt* magazine. He was saying he didn't see why he should be in their magazine, which was a benefit to them. "If they want the information they should buy my book."

Being approached by outsiders who wanted to get him to grow the IKKA he said he was happy with having a small group. I don't think he held onto that. It seemed to me he was on a quest to grow the association in the early 80s though.

The change to the 24 technique curriculum and addition of sets was discussed. "I'm just toying with it." He added, "32 is a hell of a lot."

Regarding forms, he said he created the short forms in a couple of days. Form Four took a bit longer. He called it Long Four.

He and Skip discussed Skip's concept of amplification, an idea which would become part of our terminology. Skip would be a big part of refining terms and constructing the 24 curriculum. "That's good thinking. As long as you stick to logic you'll come up with good answers." He reminded us we would be self-correcting if we understood the logic.

I had questions on some techniques in the green material. Here I was to ask about differences in what was in the manual and what Trejo taught me. Mr. Parker clarified what he was illustrating in those techniques. He also asked to see the manual, something he would do in my lessons and indicated that he, like many of us, would not always rely on memory. "Those are all the technical questions I have right now". "You have non-technical questions?" he said with a chuckle.

Private Lesson

November 1981

This lesson was two years into my studies with him. I'd seen him about every three months since November 1979 and he came to my school twice a year for seminars. We talked on the phone a lot. The conversation between us is much more relaxed, I was not as intimidated. We'd gotten to know each other, would trade jokes, laugh and one of my students said he could tell we were friends.

He reiterated full range of motion for beginners, talking about Long Form One. As you progress you can condense motion but you need a point of reference.

We discussed the "Incorrect cover" step in Short Two between the upward block/middle-knuckle sections. He told me he was glad I brought it up because he now knew it needed to be included in the book. It was intended to be an example of possibilities of handling environmental considerations.

I asked about the original self-defense techniques, were they like what we do today? He said most of what he changed or added was foot positions and leg checks.

He spent several minutes reading about the development of Kenpo, words that would find their way into *Infinite Insights*. He traced the Mitose lineage, spoke of the influence of the Chinese in Hawai'i and the mainland, Tong wars and Karate Kenpo, the original name of our system. "Kenpo is purely an art of self-defense." He continued that Chow got the Chinese martial art influence from his father and the Japanese from Mitose.

Listening to him reading me his manuscript for *Infinite Insights into Kenpo, Volume 1* brought back pleasant memories, hearing him tell the story in his own voice.

We went back to technical questions. I had observed that interlocking fingers to strike with two hands actually slowed one down in effecting a release and he agreed. I see people do it in *Blinding Sacrifice*, not good.

With the questions I asked about techniques I explained what I was thinking and he agreed with me. I was glad to hear the affirmations.

I had been at the Pasadena studio Friday night technique line the night before and mentioned how I had picked up good variations on the techniques from Yosh Furuya, Roger

Meadows, Paul Dye and many others. I told him Trejo's upcoming crop of black belt candidates were looking good and he said he meant to come down to watch them but got held up. Those four would include Paul Girard, Steve Orcino, John Murillo and Paul Casey. Paul Girard would later become the head instructor at Pasadena about 10 years later and Paul Casey would found the Kenpo Karate Hall of Fame.

Afterword

Around 1980 I lived in my studio for a short time. I can tell you I've met others who have done the same thing. We were young, hopeful "karate guys", or "karate bums", if you prefer. I had a pull-out couch in the office, and a shower, which was more than some had. Many of us were used to sleeping on the mat, or a couch, something I saw at Pasadena frequently. I slept on the mat there myself days before the IKC some years. I brought Mr. Parker to Chicago for the first time around this time and he wanted to see the studio. He said seeing where I was talking from gave him a better sense of things. I guess he pictured me sitting at my desk.

I did not go to learn from him with the thought that someday I'd be the big shot, the high-rank, the lineage head, the next Ed Parker. I went to learn. I met the late Jim Mitchell around then and he had his hair cut and colored like Ed Parker's, practiced his mannerisms and even told me "I want to be Ed Parker." Not me, I was never going to be Ed Parker. I wanted to be the best Lee I could be.

I've written in other books about what he taught us about the martial arts. With this book I hope you've been able to see there was so much more to him. He opened doors for me that brought me to where I am today. I mention many of the names of those I met in my years with him in this book and my others. Some of those other names are Bryan Hawkins, Howard Silva, Sam Babikian, Goldie Mack, Jack Farr, Jack Autry, Gary Swan, Brian Duffy, Paul Mills, Chuck Sullivan, Bob White, Ron Chapel, Rainer Schulte, Barbara Hale, Dian Tanaka, Jaime Sainz, Andy Guzman, Jeff Speakman, Larry Tatum, Roy MacDonald, Jaki McVicar, Mervyn Ormand, Charlie Gonzalez, Rich Hale, Danny Inosanto, Vic LeRoux, Gilbert Velez, Paul Mills, Dave Hebler, David Stanley, Remy Presas, Tadashi Yamashita, Fumio Demura, Larry Hartsell, Prof. Danny Lee, Tommy Chavies, John Conway Jr and Sr., Lorcan Carey, Gino Fusciardi, Benny "The Jet" Urquidez, Chuck Norris and more. I met, talked with and learned with and from them.

Ed Parker gave me insights into karate politics and human nature. He warned and informed me about accepting awards and recognition from groups and associations. "They'll want to point at you for legitimacy." In later years I'd be asked to support a group and I considered whether I needed them or they needed me and his advice when I made a decision. When I'd tell him it was time to start a seminar he'd say "Let them wait", a showbiz tactic. In my travels with him I got a much-needed education about a variety of cultures. In Australia at a tournament, I saw a man do a gesture to him every time they passed, bringing his open hand up to the contour of is nose, right palm facing left and lowering his head. When I mimicked it later, Mr. Parker said "Don't make fun of them, it's their culture, a sign of respect" and told me more about how Polynesians interact with higher-ups, particularly royalty. I was a rough kid from the South Side of Chicago and he knew I needed some polish.

He was instrumental in the success of my studio. I was taught about business, handling problem students and unusual situations. I find myself doing that for school owners today. It would be just a few years into the 1980s that a few school owners read some business books and applied what they learned. The industry took off. Running a studio is not easy and back then one with 100 students was rare. It was hungry, young people like me that kept at it and many of us became successful. His reputation helped me, and not just knowledge and business-wise.

A man came into my studio one afternoon, with two more in tow. I recognized him. He had a reputation for physically challenging instructors. Being alone and outnumbered I thought "It's my turn. I can't hold back."

He looked around, saw the IKKA crest on the wall, asked me, "Are you one of Ed Parker's boys?" I said yes, he stuck out his hand and introduced himself. I invited them in, we talked and laughed and whenever I saw him at a tournament he'd stop what he was doing and bow. The Parker lesson of "Let a handshake and a smile be your weapons" was great advice.

Toward the end of the decade the industry as a whole was having problems and I was told that 25% of the studios in the US closed. Century Martial Art Supplies even closed distribution centers. That's when I moved into a racquet club to teach part-time and took a day job as a flight instructor. Full-time karate wasn't working on the blue-collar South Side. I missed the 1989 IKC and would not see my teacher until November 1990 when I brought him in for what would be his last seminar for us and he would promote me to sixth, eleven years after I started my Lessons with Ed Parker.

In the 90s, after he'd passed, there was fragmenting of the IKKA but seminar events were also held with the hopes of cementing the people in the system and perpetuating the art. Ed Parker had been the glue that held the IKKA together. His being gone and not having formally designated a successor contributed to the splits. In those years, Edmund Jr. gave me one of his father's gi tops. He told me he wanted me to have it, adding that he heard what his father said after hanging up the phone with so many. He said his Dad always had good things to say about me. And that was not true of some he had a call with. In 2023, I met Graham Knowles for the first time. In a lengthy and interesting conversation on many topics he told me something Ed Parker told him that I had never heard, which was that I was one of his best. It meant a lot to hear it, even after so many years after his passing.

About the Author

Lee Wedlake is a first generation Ed Parker black belt. Along with his ten books on Kenpo and years of martial arts magazine articles, his work was included in Parker's *Infinite Insights into Kenpo* series of books. He wrote the preface to Volume Three of the series, was used as the model for the forms in Volume Five, and is named in the acknowledgments in Volumes One and Five. His biography is included in two of *The Journey* books by Tom Bleecker, a compilation of the life stories of some of "the most proficient practitioners" of Parker Kenpo. Lee wrote the chapter on Kenpo for Svinth and Green's *Martial Arts of the World*.

He was inducted into the Kenpo Karate Hall of Fame in 2016, the Illinois State Hall of Fame, and The Master's Hall of Fame, which also awarded him the Mike Stone Leadership Award.

In 1980 he was named as the first-ever Parker Kenpo stylist to earn a spot in the National Top Ten in men's black belt forms. Wedlake served as the Midwest representative for Parker's International Kenpo Karate Association (IKKA) from 1979 until 1990. The IKKA also named him to their Board of Examiners after Parker's passing. He later came to act as senior advisor to Progressive Kenpo Systems (PKS), a group of Kenpo studios spanning the globe. His experience in other martial arts includes instructor certification and expertise in Russian Systema and Yang Tai Chi (Cheng Man-Ching style).

His instructor certifications in other fields include American Red Cross First Aid, CPR, AED, Blood Borne Pathogens and First Aid for Severe Trauma and Basic Life Support courses. He's also a National Rifle Association pistol instructor and Range Safety Officer.

As a Certificated Flight Instructor (CFIAIME) he holds a prestigious "Gold Seal" on his license from the Federal Aviation Administration (FAA) in single and multi-engine aircraft and has earned a Master CFI designation from the National Association of Flight Instructors, one of only 600 in the United States. He was also a volunteer Aviation Safety Counselor for the FAA. Lt. Colonel Wedlake was a member of the Civil Air Patrol, the auxiliary of the United States Air Force; in which he functioned as Florida Wing Standardization and Evaluation Officer, check pilot examiner and search and rescue (SAR) pilot. Lee was also a certified proctor for Mensa, the High IQ Society. And he's a Kentucky Colonel, having received the highest award that state gives to civilians, and is also an Admiral in the Texas Navy Association.

Lee worked in law enforcement and security and was a Lieutenant of the Alamo Rangers, the security force at the famous Alamo in San Antonio, Texas. He has taken off his badge, hung up his gun belt and retired.

Resources

www.kenpotv.com

www.vimeo.com

www.ingramcontent.com/pod-product-compliance
Lightning Source LLC
Chambersburg PA
CBHW041304110526
44590CB00028B/4237